FOREIGN POLICY
in CHRISTIAN PERSPECTIVE

Books by John C. Bennett

FOREIGN POLICY IN CHRISTIAN PERSPECTIVE

CHRISTIANS AND THE STATE

CHRISTIAN ETHICS AND SOCIAL POLICY

Edited by John C. Bennett

NUCLEAR WEAPONS AND THE CONFLICT
  OF CONSCIENCE

FOREIGN POLICY
in CHRISTIAN PERSPECTIVE

John Coleman Bennett

CHARLES SCRIBNER'S SONS, *NEW YORK*

To Anne, beloved partner and often my conscience on issues discussed in this book.

CONTENTS

PREFACE

This book is an expansion of a series of lectures which I gave
in July 1965 at an Institute on Christianity and World Affairs at
American University in Washington, D.C. The Institute was
sponsored by both the School of International Service of that University and the Department of International Affairs of the National Council of Churches of Christ in America. I am very
grateful to Dean Ernest S. Griffith for the stimulus which his invitation provided to put these ideas on paper while they may still
be relevant.

I realize that in many ways the selection of subjects that I discuss is arbitrary. For example, many readers will note with regret
that I have said nothing about the continuing crises in South
Africa and Rhodesia. I have stressed the issues with which I have
been personally most preoccupied for some years. Also, it may well
be thought that the Christian perspective is explicit in only one
chapter, but I hope that the degree to which it is implicit in the
other chapters will be evident to the reader.

I have had to trespass on the territory of a variety of experts,
and the mixture that I offer may seem pretentious. Yet, wherever
one stands, if he thinks about the complicated issues of foreign
policy, he can hardly avoid this. Theological and ethical judgments are combined with what may be more precarious judgments
about historical trends. I have made many factual or technical
statements on the authority of others, and I have made many prudential judgments as an observer of events concerning the probable effects of various policies or actions. When I first wrote chapter four, "The Cold War and Beyond," it seemed to be highly
controversial, but today most of what I say in that chapter
about European Communism has come to be more widely ac-

9

cepted, partly because there is a tendency to think favorably of the Soviet Union and the eastern European countries in comparison with Communist China. As I write, the war in Vietnam is the source of graver concern than any other problem related to foreign policy. Much that I say is indirectly related to this problem but I do not want the book as a whole to be tied to the changing events in Vietnam. However, I have added a postscript to Chapter Four, which sets forth my view of this tragic conflict as the book goes to press. I hope that we may soon see more light in this situation and that this postscript may soon be out of date.

I am grateful to the Council of Religion and International Affairs for permission to modify and use in this book many passages in my pamphlet published by the Council entitled "Moral Tensions in International Affairs." This pamphlet was a paper that was discussed by two of the Council's seminars in Washington, D.C., and I learned a great deal from those occasions. Also, some passages about the changes in Communism in Chapter four appeared first in an article in *Concern* (September 1, 1965).

I want to thank the Reverend John C. Raines, Tutor in Christian Ethics at Union Theological Seminary, for reading the manuscript and for making many helpful suggestions.

JOHN C. BENNETT

February 1966
Union Theological Seminary
New York City

1: Foreign Policy as a Problem for Christian Ethics

THERE ARE many reasons why foreign policy creates acute problems for Christian ethics, indeed for any sensitive and humane ethics. Yet, Christians and others who have similar ethical concerns must continually make decisions in this area. They struggle as citizens and as policy-makers to find the best, or the least destructive, policy open to them. There are no Christian foreign policies, but Christians should be moved and guided by their faith and commitment to seek the best policies in the circumstances.

I am not sure which is worse: to claim that the policies and actions of one's nation have a special Christian sanction; or to affirm a double standard which leaves all that one does on behalf of the nation, or all to which one consents in the behavior of the nation, outside the sphere in which Christian moral convictions are relevant. In either case, the nation in relation to other nations escapes rigorous Christian criticism.

The distance between Christian ethics and foreign policy is realized fully by some policy-makers, and they agonize over it. Others who may also be men of good will and sincerity seem to be able to make the most problematic decisions without losing a night's sleep; I have in mind one such American statesman who affirmed more than once that his policy was based on the Sermon on the Mount. There are both types of Christians in the church, and my hope is that the first type will find in the church some understanding of why there is so much moral conflict in life and will receive healing for their spirits and that the second type will become more disturbed than usual when they go to church.

In an episode in the life of President Kennedy, there was a revelation of the depths of the personal problem of those who make policy. Dr. Franklin Clark Fry told about this in a broadcast on the Sunday after Kennedy's death. He had gone with a delegation from the World Council of Churches to see the President and to present to him a message to heads of states from the New Delhi Assembly of the Council. The message included a paragraph calling for the cessation of nuclear tests. This was early in 1962, before the United States had resumed nuclear tests in response to the Russian tests and more than a year before the partial test ban treaty. When Mr. Kennedy read this paragraph, he revealed his own dilemma (articles about Kennedy since his death have emphasized the depth of his concern about nuclear tests and his great satisfaction over the partial test ban treaty) and he evidently spoke with great feeling. One of the Americans in the delegation said to him: "Mr. President, if you do resume tests, how can we help you?" The President turned to him and said: "Perhaps you shouldn't." This episode illustrates the distance between what a sincere statesman may believe he must do for the sake of national security and his ethical sensitivities, indeed his normal human concerns. The worst thing that the church could have done would have been to give a Christian sanction to nuclear testing. Kennedy evidently wanted criticism to be kept alive. Those who must act in the political realm should keep listening for criticism and fresh guidance from the ethical realm. Even their assumptions, which at one time may be correct, need to be continually reassessed. Why is the distance so great between foreign policy and Christian ethics?

It is not enough to invoke the Christian understanding of the finiteness and sin of man in abstract and general terms. Nations have moral problems and temptations of a peculiar intensity. Reinhold Niebuhr's chapter, "The Morality of Nations," in his *Moral Man and Immoral Society,* is a classic statement of the situation. There are two emphases in his discussion that need to be continually repeated. One is that the very loyalty and altruism of the individual citizen, which give him moral satisfaction as a person, tend to support his nation's most characteristic sins, its prideful ambition, its greed, and its will to power. As Niebuhr puts it, "Patriotism transmutes individual unselfishness into national egoism." [1] Also he emphasizes the tendency of nations, including the United States, to clothe the national will with idealistic pretensions. He says that "perhaps the most significant moral characteristic of a nation is hypocrisy," and he notes that this hypocrisy is "the tribute which immorality pays to morality." [2] To recognize this is to avoid cynicism, but the moral confusion remains. During the Second World War, Archbishop William Temple used to say that one difference between the British and the Nazis was that the former did not practice what they preached, but the latter did. It is better to keep the sources of moral judgment alive in the national life at the cost of hypocrisy than it is to lower the proclaimed standards to the practice of the moment. However, the use of morality to justify whatever the nation does may lead to a rigid or fanatical self-righteousness.

The capacity of a nation for self-deception is endless. Its claims to righteousness are used to clothe any actions to which it may be led, especially in times of stress. In an age of ideology, this tendency is aggravated. And in so far as there is an element of truth in a nation's moral claims, it is difficult for citizens to protect themselves against self-deceptions. In times of crisis, when national debate may be limited by considerations of patriotism and national security, the moral problem created by such self-deception is compounded. Professor Herbert Butterfield is one of the chief interpreters of the destructive effects of frenzied national self-righteousness. He makes much of the idea that the most furious and cruel conflicts are conflicts among what he calls "giant organized systems of self-righteousness" with each system only too delighted to find that the other is wicked—each only too glad that the sins give it the pretext for still deeper hatred and animosity. [3]

There is much emphasis on the same point in the writings of George Kennan and Walter Lippmann. Together with Butterfield they trace the absolute self-righteousness of total war to the

---

[1] Charles Scribner's Sons, 1932, p. 91.   [2] *Ibid.*, p. 95.
[3] *Christianity, Diplomacy and War*, Abingdon Press, 1953, p. 43.

need of mobilizing democracies for combat. Kennan says of the First World War: "There is, let me assure you, nothing more egocentrical than the embattled democracy. It soon becomes the victim of its own war propaganda. It then tends to attach to its own cause an absolute value which distorts its own vision on everything else. *Its* enemy becomes the embodiment of all evil. *Its* own side, on the other hand, is the center of all virtue." [4] It is well to recall that Kennan is thinking of the war against the Germany of the Kaiser, a moderate compared with later enemies. Lippmann makes the same point: "When the world wars came, the people of the liberal democracies could not be aroused to the exertions and the sacrifices of the struggle until they had been frightened by the opening disasters, had been incited to passionate hatred, and had become intoxicated with unlimited hope. . . . The people wanted to be told that when this particular enemy had been forced to unconditional surrender, they would re-enter the golden age." [5]

All of this, when generalized, could lead to very simple moral judgments. Christian citizens moved by this picture of nations might simply say of any conflict between nations: "a plague on all houses" and hold themselves aloof from all the policies of their own nation. But this is no answer. Nations are the only units of power that can do many things that need to be done. They have responsibility to act commensurate with their power. National ideals may not be merely rationalizations of crude national interests or expressions of national self-righteousness. Whatever the self-deceptions of the United States, it was not wrong about the threat of Hitlerism to humanity and it was not wrong about the need to develop power in the defense of Europe against Stalinism. In the first case, it allowed what was right in its cause to hide the recklessness of the policy of unconditional surrender, and in the second case, it may have exaggerated the danger of a direct military attack on Western Europe. The United States is right today in trying to keep as much of the world as possible

---

[4] *Russia and the West under Lenin and Stalin,* Little Brown & Co., 1960, pp. 5-6.
[5] *The Public Philosophy,* Little Brown & Co., 1955, p. 21.

open so that nations can choose their own social systems, though today it does exaggerate the role of military force in this effort, and it clothes its policies with far too simple ideas of freedom and with a too absolutistic anti-Communism. What the United States did to help the nations of Europe rebuild their economies after the war represented an admirable combination of humanitarian concern and an enlightened interpretation of national interest. I mention these matters, some of which will be discussed later, to emphasize the error in a cynical criticism of American foreign policy.

These peculiar temptations of nations are enhanced and become the more destructive in an international situation that lacks any effective system of law or collective security. This lack causes the major powers to prepare to defend themselves against all real or potential enemies. The objective situation of mutual mistrust compounds the sin of all. In the case of both the American and the Soviet effort to achieve security, each nation tries to prepare itself against all possible as well as all probable dangers. It is the professional responsibility of a department of defense to prepare for the worst and to take seriously the possible though improbable dangers beyond the point of common sense in other contexts. In this atmosphere of mistrust, fears for survival are used to justify preparations that, if the worst comes to the worst, can destroy the cities and the very substance of another nation. This preparation for murderous deeds, which are now regarded as a last resort, is also rationalized with some plausibility by the assumption that it will actually prevent the very war in which the nation might be driven to them. At least that assumption enables citizens who retain ordinary humane sentiments to live with their preparations for limitless violence.

In addition to the temptations with which nations live that are exaggerations of the temptations that generally belong to the human situation, there are elements of the structure of nations and of international relations that, in themselves morally neutral, create grave moral perplexities.

The fact that a government must act as a trustee for a nation, for a secular nation with very mixed opinions and with a strong bias in favor of narrow national interests, limits what the policy-maker may do and what the citizen may expect. Governments are responsible to the people of the nation and they are responsible for the real interests, including the military security, of their nations. The Christian statesman is bound by these responsibilities, though he may go far in leading his nation to take a far-sighted and humane view of its interests and to recognize quite generally the common interests shared with other nations. In a later chapter, I shall discuss the moral issues raised by the claims of national interest. There is some flexibility here, and the churches can do a great deal to enable their members to take a broad view of national interest and to transcend it in their personal convictions and commitments. However, they should recognize how limited the alternatives confronting a statesman may be, and avoid self-righteousness in criticizing him.

Perhaps the most widely recognized limitation of Christian ethics, indeed of ethics as such, in the sphere of foreign policy comes from the mixture of moral and technical elements in the necessary decisions.

There are technical elements in foreign policy known only to experts; there are also matters of political wisdom that may not be technical in the narrow sense but that depend upon specialized experience, on being on the spot and living closely with a problem in all its changing details. Not only is there relevant information, sometimes classified information, available to a small group of experts, there is also a high degree of technical competence required in judging the effect of any policy upon the relative power of a nation, and hence upon its future security. Foreign policy is based in large measure on educated guesses concerning the effect of a decision upon the attitudes and behavior of other nations. Guesses about what may happen in the Soviet Union, or in China, or in the noncommitted world are essential. How much truth is there in the "domino theory" in relation to the problems of South East Asia? That is a problem that calls for knowledge of the region as well as for some general knowledge of the behavior of nations as units of power. It also calls for understanding of the dynamics of Communism at various stages. To ask the man in the street or the man in the church for an off-the-cuff judgment on such matters cannot produce much enlightenment.

All discussions of arms control or disarmament or of the use of particular weapons in war involve both moral and technical considerations. Ultimately, the questions of what risks should be taken are moral questions. The questions concerning the nature and extent of the risks are technical or political questions. The vast subject of weaponry, which fills the current books about national security and national strategy, is remote from the training of the student of Christian ethics and of most leaders of the church, but Christian teaching cannot be related to the issues of military policy unless there is knowledge about such matters. Professor Paul Ramsey, in his many writings about the ethics of war in the nuclear age, has done good service in learning his way about the current discussions of weapons and strategy.[6] Wishing this world of weaponry away does no good. Christian judgments about the use of various weapons are in order, but such judgments are not independent of other judgments that are made concerning their effects, concerning the alternatives in the spectrum of weapons, concerning the probable effects of renouncing their use.

In most moral decisions there is an inherent difficulty, which takes acute forms in international affairs because of the size and complexity of the problems involved. The citizens of a nation find themselves seeking two or more objectives, each one of which may have a valid moral claim upon them but which are in tension or even in conflict with each other. When this is the case there may be no overriding moral criterion by which such a conflict can be adjudicated. Today we may easily recognize conflicts of this sort between peace and freedom or between justice and order.

---

[6] Professor Ramsey has written the most substantial American book on the ethics of war in the nuclear age, *War and the Christian Conscience,* Duke University Press, 1961. He has also returned to this problem in many articles and pamphlets, especially his chapter in *Nuclear Weapons and the Conflict of Conscience,* ed. J. C. Bennett, Charles Scribner's Sons, 1962, and in two pamphlets published by the Council on Religion and International Affairs, his own pamphlet, "The Limits of Nuclear War," and, "Peace, the Churches and the Bomb," of which he is one of the authors.

Considered abstractly, these values are actually interdependent, and conflicts between them are provisional, and yet most of the honest bafflement about policy comes from the effort to do justice to two or more goals that call for different emphases related to these values. In the period of the Cold War, the United States has been concerned to prevent the imposition of Communism by one country on another and thus to preserve as wide an area of freedom to choose as possible. It has also been concerned to prevent war, especially nuclear war. If it could have concentrated on one of these objectives and ignored the other, decisions would have been relatively simple. I think it is fair to say that the government of the United States has really been committed to both objectives, though there are segments of public opinion which subordinate one to the other so completely that they evade the dilemmas involved.

There is another difficulty of quite a different sort, and the last to be discussed here: the current revulsion against "moralism" in the attitude of nations. I use the word "moralism" to indicate two types of thinking: the use of moral slogans and stereotypes apart from the complicated context of moral choice, and the assumption that all problems will yield to moral suasion, if only it is pushed with greater intensity. Moralism in the form of one-sided stereotypes is the stuff of self-righteousness, and it inspires propaganda against adversaries, dividing the world between righteous and unrighteous nations. This is widely criticized as a characteristic American tendency, but Americans have no monopoly of it. There is an absolutistic moralism characteristic of the Communist nations in their attacks on "imperialism."

Until recently, there were great pressures in many Christian circles to make the Cold War a holy crusade against Communist nations as godless and immoral foes. The World Council of Churches and other ecumenical movements in the Protestant-Orthodox world have generally avoided this stance, but there was a tendency for Roman Catholics to war on Communism in this spirit. We owe to Pope John, more than to anyone else, a debt of gratitude for the fact that the non-Communist nations, and especially those under Christian influence, are moving away from the "holy war" psychology. Moralistic or religious crusading of any kind may make impossible the compromises and accommodations without which nations cannot live together on this planet. Using "democracy" as a moralistic criterion by which we judge all other nations is a source of confusion. The American attitude toward neutrals during the earlier stages of the Cold War was in part a result of the habit of drawing our own moral lines without first seeking to understand the motives and special needs of other nations. Moralistic foreign policies usually produce devils on the other side, and it is hard to negotiate with devils, though without negotiations there may be no future for them or for us. The revulsion against moralism may cause many critics to be afraid of talking about morality in relation to foreign policy at all, but this is a mistake. This very revulsion is itself favorable to a more sensitive understanding of morality, one that sees humility as an essential national virtue and that is influenced by a charitable openness to the neighbor, even when the neighbor is an adversary.

So far, I have emphasized obstacles to the relating of Christian ethics to foreign policy. These obstacles do not destroy the relevance of Christian ethics to this area of our life, but they do set some of the conditions which surround the thinking and vocation of Christians. The fact that there is no Christian policy changes in no way the moral responsibility to make the most of what margin of freedom one has to serve all the neighbors within reach, to seek for the nation goals that are just and humane, and, when the going is roughest, to prevent the greater evil.

After one has discounted all the self-justifying moralistic propganda with which national leaders surround their policies, one must still affirm the national responsibilities that have moral significance. Some possibilities open to the nation are more consistent with a Christian or humane ethic than others. For this reason it is wrong to leave foreign policy to the devil or to the expert who denies the relevance of moral concerns. I have already mentioned such objectives as an open world and the conditions of peace. When I discuss national interest, I shall have much to say about the American national interest in the welfare of other nations and in a reasonable stability in the international situation, though not in a *status quo* rigidly protected against all radical change.

The Christian may have a vocation as a policy-maker and as a citizen of his nation interested in foreign policy. Even when the choice may be between evils that seem very dark, the choice may still have positive meaning for his Christian vocation. Not to choose, or to withdraw, may have disastrous effects, which he seeks to prevent. There are times when almost any order is better than anarchy. There are also times when Christians may be right in engaging in civil disobedience or revolution against the only order available at the moment in the hope that such action may make possible a better order. But there is always a burden of proof on decisions for civil disobedience or withdrawal.

Also, there should be great emphasis on moral restraints in the means used. These restraints may not always prevail when pressure becomes too great, but moral criticism within government itself as well as from citizens in general has some effect. Without trying to defend any particular policy, I am arguing here only against those who think in terms of a separation between policy and morality, which makes the latter irrelevant. One of the most significant examples of restraint was the decision, during the Cuban crisis in October 1962, not to bomb the missile bases. At each stage of the crisis, President Kennedy chose to take action that was as limited as possible, given the objective. At the time, it was revealed, definitely moral arguments were used against a direct strike at Cuba. In an ethic of means, the moral interest and the dictates of prudence are intertwined.

Restraints in the use of power stem from mixed motives, and today the chief motive may be to avoid provoking a dangerous response from the Soviet Union; yet for many individuals involved in making policy there is a genuine concern for the people who might be injured or destroyed by less restrained action.

Dean Acheson, in a famous speech on morality and policy, made many good points about the misuse of simple moral maxims as guides to policy, but he appeared to go too far in declaring the

moral autonomy of what he called "the strategic approach." [7]
This does not stand by itself. Its objectives, I am sure he would
admit, are subject to moral criticism more sophisticated than the
application of maxims. I believe he created a wrong impression in
saying that "those involved in the Cuban crisis of October 1962
will remember the irrelevance of the supposed moral considerations brought out in the discussion." Moral considerations as
detached absolutes may have been irrelevant, but particular
moral objections to a direct strike against missile sites were attributed at the time to Robert Kennedy.[8] But apart from such objections, which were specifically moral in a somewhat narrow
sense, morality is involved in all prudential judgments that seek
to avoid the greater evil and all its human consequences.

Even when Mr. Acheson announces the great goal of policy "to
preserve and foster an environment in which free societies may
exist and flourish," he himself makes use of a one-sided moralistic
phrase in speaking of "free societies." How freedom and a transforming social justice and viability and order are to be related
in a period of tumultuous change raises problems of morals and
strategy, for which his own prescriptions are too simple.

I have made much of the obstacle to the application of morality
to foreign policy coming from the emphasis upon the expert and
the man on the spot who have special knowledge and experience.
But they are moral beings. Their consciences have already been
formed, and, while nothing may be done to change them in an

---

[7] This speech was delivered at Amherst College, December 9, 1964. Quotations
are from excerpts in *The New York Times* of December 10th.

[8] Max Frankel in *The New York Times* wrote about "the general feeling that
a surprise attack would be contrary to the country's traditions, history and
aspirations, that it would be a response not commensurate with the provocation and that it would permanently damage the president's ability to promote
responsible conduct in international affairs." (Oct. 30, 1962.) A more extensive report in *The New York Times*, Nov. 3, 1962, confirmed this report
and mentioned that Attorney General Robert Kennedy emphasized the moral
grounds for avoiding an attack on the Cuban missile bases. This is also reported by Arthur Schlesinger, Jr., *A Thousand Days*, Houghton Mifflin, 1965,
pp. 806-7.

emergency, what has gone into the formation of their consciences may be very fateful. The outsider at the moment may not have relevant guidance. He is shut out from classified information, and he is removed from the immediate contact with the most pressing realities. And yet, in a relatively free society, outsiders have a responsibility to keep reminding insiders of values that they may forget when they are immersed in any immediate crisis.

If we look away from the limited emergency to the broader operation to which the insiders are committed, such insiders as the President and the Secretary of State and the Secretary of Defense and other trusted advisers, I seriously question whether their judgments are determined, except in very limited areas of tactics and timing, as much by the classified information or other specialized knowledge to which they have access as they are by their broad pictures of the world. Today such a group of insiders are very much influenced by their ideas about the dynamics of Communism, about the role of military power in relation to the containment of Communism in a revolutionary situation, about the relation of revolution in various countries to American conceptions of freedom and to American security, about the extent of the risks of nuclear war and the moral right of the United States to take these risks, about the range of American responsibilities and the limits of American power, about many intangible factors in other cultures, and about the effect of what we do on the attitudes of other peoples. Convictions about these and similar matters are more determinative than information on which such policy-makers may have a monopoly. Such convictions are already influenced by moral ideas, often by very conventional American "moralisms," often by much talk of "honor," as they determine policy today. All of these convictions belong to the sphere of public debate to which Christian ethics is relevant. Also, ethical sensitivities that come from the experience of the universal church should have an effect on this debate, for one of the chief sources of correction of the stereotypes that do such heavy duty in molding public opinion on these matters is openness to the needs and aspirations and fears and interpretations of people in other nations.

There is one special danger that should be noted, and that is the danger that one easily identified form of expertise may do duty for others. For example, those who know a great deal about the military aspects of a policy often dogmatize about these broader issues, especially about the dynamics of Communism and about the role of China. All that they say carries weight because they are experts on elements of the problem which they discuss. And yet the validity of their recommendations depends chiefly on conventional generalizations in areas outside the field about which they can speak with authority. This is true of many declarations of policy by Secretary MacNamara, of the writings about Asian policy by Hanson Baldwin. One of the most extreme examples is the book by General Patrick W. Powers, formerly head of the Strategic Air Command, dealing with American policy in Asia.[9]

The experts of experts on matters of strategy are often those engaged in intelligence work. The secrecy of their operations makes it impossible for any outsider to judge their credentials. But the C.I.A. on important occasions, notably in connection with the episode of the Bay of Pigs and in connection with the intervention in the Dominican Republic in 1965, has shown a very strong bias in its fact-finding. More than any other agency of government, it seems to be controlled by an absolutistic form of anti-Communism, even though individual C.I.A officials may have a sound grasp of world politics. It seems to have a pathological fear of all revolutions. It was certainly governed by wishful thinking in its estimate of what was taking place in Cuba in the spring of 1961. It is no wonder President Kennedy wished he had not trusted these experts at that time.[10]

Often the argument that is supposed to settle the issues of the relevance of ethics to foreign policy is that moral debate on these issues in a crisis is likely to give a wrong signal to the adversaries. They may assume that the American people are divided, or are not resolute about their announced policies, because many Americans are known to have moral scruples. Moral criticism in time

---

[9] *Guide to National Defense,* Praeger, 1963.
[10] Theodore Sorenson, *Kennedy,* Harper and Row, 1965, p. 309.

of conflict is believed to be debilitating for a nation. This view of the matter has often been pressed in recent years in connection with the Cuban crisis and in connection with American actions in South East Asia. It really asks the citizens to declare a moratorium on moral criticism of policy during an emergency.

The press, the universities, and the churches are criticized when they are sources of criticism of established policies. But, from the point of view of the insiders who try to pursue a balanced policy, silence on the part of such critics should not be desired, for these policy-makers in any case will be pressed by the more nationalistic and the more belligerent segments of opinion, by those who give chief emphasis to military solutions, by those who are controlled by the more simplistic and absolutistic forms of anti-Communism. Policy-makers should learn from experience that they may even be imprisoned at a later time by a public opinion which they have helped to make intransigent. This has happened in the United States in the case of China policy.

It is essential that there be open criticism of policies and strategies by those who emphasize restraint, by those who believe that goals should be limited, by those who see how the world appears to people on other continents. Quite apart from this practical need of balancing forces within this country, it is morally impossible for citizens who share the concerns emphasized in this book to be silent.

There is one ethical test of foreign policy that is implied throughout this discussion, but it needs to be made explicit. The foreign policy of states should be favorable to morally sensitive, personal living with people across national boundaries. One of the chief evils of political totalitarianism is that it allows no independent, moral basis for personal relations with people in other countries. One of the morally intolerable aspects of war is that it not only turns people into destroyers of their neighbors on the other side of a conflict but in many other ways renders impossible truthful human communication and personal relationships. It tends to destroy the moral claims of persons who are for the moment enemies. One very admirable episode in recent French history was the organized revulsion in France against the use of torture by French troops in Algeria.[11] Especially repellent are policies of states that cause citizens to defy their own moral sensitivities in dealing with other persons because of a political relationship with them.[11]

In this country, we have usually solved this problem by having an ethic of war that has permitted great barbarities against people, especially people at a distance, and an ethic of peace that in principle enabled us to deal with persons as persons regardless of political relationships. The ethic of war was put in brackets, and it was assumed to be exceptional. Indeed, when peace returned, we would build up the cities destroyed by our side during the war. This neat division between an ethic of war and an ethic of peace has been lost to a considerable extent in a time of Cold War, revolution, and civil conflict, but policy-makers and citizens still have a responsibility to reduce to a minimum the practices that corrupt or destroy personal relations.

Except for an occasional revelation that causes one to be suspicious of all that remains unrevealed, I do not know what is being done by American secret agents. There is a moral underworld below the acknowledged ambiguities and compromises of international relations that—whether necessary or not under present conditions of international insecurity and conflict—should not be allowed to exist without moral restraints. The citizen should be able to know that some trustworthy persons are in a position to insist on the preservation of moral limits in this underworld. The fact of the President's ultimate responsibility is reassuring

[11] I have been surprised that there has been so little sense of outrage in this country in relation to the torturing of prisoners by our Vietnamese allies. It is true that General Westmoreland sent out a fine order to American troops about the treatment of prisoners but there is too much complacency in the face of a situation which causes James Reston to say: "The brutality of the Vietnamese to the fellow countrymen they capture is almost beyond our comprehension." (*The New York Times*, January 23, 1966) We cannot escape moral involvement in this cruelty since the Vietnamese army depends so much on American support. Also, this is one illustration of the double standard that Americans apply so often that causes them to cite continually the atrocities of their adversaries and to forget so quickly the atrocities of their friends.

to some extent, but he is finite, and this underworld may get out from under his control. When the visible leaders lie to protect the underworld, one wonders how much this corrupts the upper world! I cannot say that this whole enterprise must be abandoned, because, objectionable as it is, in a world without reliable instruments of collective security, the activity of this kind of intelligence agency, *if it is not an independent initiator of policy,* may be a crude substitute for recognized international institutions of inspection that are intended to reduce the actual insecurity of nations.

One of the consequences of the Cold War that needs to be kept under moral scrutiny is the absence of relationships between Americans as such and the people of whole nations, especially China and Cuba. This utter denial of human relationships across national boundaries is itself a great evil and not to be accepted complacently as the result of some political necessity. One other example of human relations affected by national policy is the situation of being a citizen of a rich nation in a poor world where most people remain hungry.

I should not conclude this chapter without facing one challenge to the positions presented in this book; it is highly relevant to the question of how problematic foreign policy is for Christian ethics. Forms of pacifism provide what may seem to be a shortcut to a Christian foreign policy or, at least, to a foreign policy that avoids the usual moral ambiguities. It would not avoid all such ambiguities, but it would prevent the most harassing moral conflicts that come from the national use of military force or the national preparation to use military force. Today there is a special form of pacifism that stresses the conviction that the use of nuclear weapons is beyond all moral limits. I shall deal with the issues created by nuclear pacifism in a later chapter. Here I shall explain in general terms my reasons for being unable to take a pacifist view of the problems of foreign policy. I shall deal only with the type of pacifism that offers a political alternative to the policy of the government; this is the most articulate form in the United States. Pacifism that intends to be the vocation of an individual or of a witnessing community that withdraws from those sectors of political life closely related to the military policies of the state is quite a different matter. This type of pacifism is most consistently represented by the Mennonites who, traditionally at least, have not claimed to have a political role. Their ideal has been to establish communities that have as much self-sufficiency as possible in relation to the surrounding political community. That even they have to choose a political community free and tolerant enough to accept them and to cooperate with their desire to preserve the status of conscientious objectors shows that they cannot be indifferent to political choices.

I shall mention two reasons for being unable to accept pacifism as the source of political answers.

The first is that no government responsible to an existing nation can adopt a policy based upon pacifist convictions. To be sure, it can choose some policies that go part way, and do so with strong pacifist support, as in the case of the achievement of the partial test ban treaty. But the non-pacifist would have to say that such an achievement came in part because each side felt threatened by the other's power. The acceptance of co-existence was in part the result of the nuclear stalemate. No nation that can have substantial military strength will allow its government to gamble with its security by disarming unilaterally, leaving it no alternative to surrendering to superior force. There are many nations today that cannot have such strength, but they depend upon the strength of allies whose interest it is to defend them. They are not pacifist nations in basic intention. A large segment of Japanese public opinion might prefer a non-military course for their nation, but this view, which is based upon a natural revulsion against Japanese militarism of the recent past, is not likely to be dominant in the long run. Moreover, Japan can hardly escape protection by American power! India was close to a pacifist creed, but even in the days of Nehru, when this view had the highest moral prestige, it was not consistently followed; the Indian government used military force to keep Hyderabad in the federal union, and it did the same to try to hold Kashmir. When India was invaded by China, it renounced all pacifist pretensions, and more recent fighting between India and Pakistan shows even more clearly how thin was the pacifism of this semi-pacifist nation.

Quite apart from arguments based upon the behavior of this or that nation, which might be a borderline case, there is no doubt whatever that the United States is not a pacifist nation, and that its government cannot escape responsibility for its military defense. I am not interested in stating the obvious facts about American use of military force now in a limited war and about its reliance for its security upon over-kill military capacity as a deterrent. My only point is that there is little in the American ethos that would make it possible for the government to renounce military force in principle.

In view of this situation, American pacifists, if they are to speak to policy-makers in terms of real possibilities, cannot recommend a pacifist policy. There is always a moral danger that pacifists in dealing with government will recommend policies that may seem on the surface to be closest to pacifism, as during the 1930s there was a tendency for political pacifists and isolationists to make common cause against participation in the Second World War. Pacifists need to guard against the temptation to play down the degree of the threat posed by another nation or group of nations in order to persuade their own nation to come as close as possible to a policy of non-violence. In so doing, they may only succeed in making their nation relatively weak, and invite aggression. Because I believe that the threat of Communist nations is much less a military threat than was that of Hitler's Germany, I often find the contribution of pacifists today a more helpful corrective than was the case in the 1930s. They play down, more than I regard as sound, the role of the deterrent capacity of the United States, but there is very little danger at the moment that this will be neglected. Pacifist groups often contribute an emphasis on constructive alternatives to military force and on efforts to re-establish relationships and to encourage reconciliation between nations, which is greatly needed. Most citizens have less freedom of mind than pacifists to concentrate on these aspects of policy. They are among the pioneers in seeing beyond the assumptions of the Cold War. Against all the pressures to conform, they have been among the most courageous citizens in keeping alive the national debate about policy in Vietnam. But it remains true that pacifism does not have a self-sufficient alternative to the government's dependence on military force.

My second reason for rejecting pacifism as the source of answers to the questions of foreign policy is that I cannot renounce the use of military power to deter a nuclear attack, to defend people from invasion or from political oppression. Whether it should be used in any particular case depends upon whether it would do more good than harm. I shall deal in later chapters with the issues that are raised here. A strong case can be made against the possession or use of nuclear weapons under any circumstances, though my discussion of that subject, in chapter five, does not quite reach that absolutistic conclusion. Quite apart from the nuclear problem, the need of possessing military power to prevent a nation from being vulnerable to attack or blackmailing pressure, in the world as it is, is clear to me.

Pacifism, as a political strategy based upon a way of life involving the avoidance of organized killing as a sin against love and involving trust in the persuasive and reconciling power of love in dealing with evil forces that threaten or oppress a community, is one Christian response to the realities of international conflict. It is the one that seems most clearly in line with the sayings about non-resistance in the gospels, and therefore many Christians have been claimed by it in every generation. I believe that prior to any such gospel sayings that can be made into a particular law of non-violence is the broader commandment of love for all neighbors. This broader commandment can be seen to involve doing what we can in some circumstances to defend neighbors against aggressors and to rescue them from oppression. These neighbors may be our fellow-citizens who depend upon the measures we and they take together as a nation for its defense, or they may be people threatened or oppressed in other nations.

It is quite possible to say that these broader implications of love are limited by particular laws that forbid the use of violence against any neighbors, even to prevent them from engaging in acts of aggression or oppression; but I doubt that this is the better interpretation of the meaning of Christian love, and, since I do not accept it, I leave the door open in principle (as most Christians have done since they gained political responsibility) to the use of military force by nations. When that door is once opened, the most harassing perplexities of foreign policy enter; we are in the midst of all of the ambiguities of how to possess and even to use military force and yet to keep it limited and restrained as the servant of justice. There is a pragmatic pacifism that is not based upon an absolute renunciation of military force or on an absolute trust in peaceful persuasion but on the calculation that in the present state of military technology, when nations use military force, they are too prone to overdo it and bring upon themselves and the world the greater evil. The case for this is very strong but not conclusive.[12] And so the following chapters

[12] I find myself quite close to the position of Karl Barth who said the following about war and pacifism in 1951: "All affirmative answers to the question [of war] are wrong if they do not start with the assumption that the inflexible negative of pacifism has almost infinite arguments in its favor and is almost overpoweringly strong." *Church Dogmatics*, Volume III, Part 4, p. 455. It is interesting to observe that, during the Second World War, Barth kept urging Christians in many countries, except his own, neutral Switzerland, to wage war ardently against Hitler on Christian grounds and that later, in the 1950s, Barth moved toward nuclear pacifism. It is a striking fact that Emil Brunner, who seldom agrees with Barth, in *The Divine Imperative* (The Westminster Press, 1947), first published in 1932, came to an even stronger conclusion against participation in war based upon the nature of modern war. He said of it: "Where war has reached this stage of development it has lost every particle of ethical justification." He went on to say: "Again, when conscientious and politically sane citizens refuse to render a service to the State which used to be considered a very real service, but has now, in their opinion, become politically useless, they show political wisdom; this is shown by the fact that they regard this refusal as the Command of God to them, not in the legalistic sense of fanatics, but in the concrete sense of political responsibility, that is, in a quite different sense from those who refuse this service simply on the ground of the command: 'Thou shalt not kill,' or on the basis of the Sermon on the Mount." (p. 475) Brunner later came to support the Second World War, and he became one of the most belligerent of all Protestant theologians in relation to Communism, approving the military policies of the Western powers, including their strategy of nuclear deterrence. But this passage, together with Barth's, shows that a tendency toward prag-

will presuppose that military power is a necessary ingredient of national power but at the same time a profound problem for Christian ethics.

---

matic pacifism is not necessarily dependent on liberal theology or on sectarian perfectionism! It reflects a change in circumstances that determines where one locates the greatest evil.

2: *The Christian Perspective*

THE NATURE of this chapter is very different from that of the preceding one. This fact illustrates the distance that I have emphasized between Christian faith and ethics on the one hand and the raw stuff of international relations on the other.

There are various overlapping contrasts with which any study in Christian social ethics must begin. There is the contrast between the public and political sphere and the sphere of personal relations that seems less resistant to Christian influences. There is the contrast between the secular world and the Christian community that is formed by its response to the distinctively Christian revelation, to which the secular world is largely indifferent. There is the contrast between church and state. I shall not try to sort out these three contrasts, but it is important to note that international relations belong to what we may regard as the outer sphere in each case. They are public and political; they belong decisively to the secular world; they involve relations between states, most of which are either indifferent or hostile to churches and all of which differ from churches in role and function.

It is important to stress one conviction about these three contrasts: no one of them from the Christian standpoint should be allowed to become a full separation. In all of them, interaction between the two spheres is real and should be increased. The political sphere has fateful effects on the personal, and part of the very substance of individuals as persons is their responsibility for what political institutions and political forces and political decisions do to their neighbors. The Christian lives in the distinctively Christian community and in the secular world. These interact in his life, and in many ways each influences the other. The Christian community should not live for itself but for the wider world; it should always be concerned about all people in that world. Church and state may be legally separate, as they are in the United States, but they are not functionally separate. Often, many moral assumptions are shared by both church and state in the nations in which there has been continuous interaction between secular forces and Christian influences. In some ways, they may be in conflict, but even in an atheistic society they share some purposes for the common welfare. The Christian citizen is always a link between church and state.

One contrast related to those mentioned is the contrast between the personal and official roles of the same individual. Luther has illumined this contrast, sometimes by exaggerating it; but again the emphasis should be on interaction rather than on separation, and what any man does officially should express or be tempered by his personal sensitivity. If there are moments when this seems impossible, he should reconsider his official role and perhaps renounce it, or do what he can to open up new possibilities for it, or find ways outside his official role to counteract the effects of some things he does in it. Luther has much to say about the Christian who is a hangman but, if there are Christian hangmen, they should work for the abolition of capital punishment.

Luther's treatise, entitled "That Soldiers, Too, Can Be Saved," states the case for the contrast of roles in the Christian life of the soldier. He writes: "When I think of the office of soldier, how it punishes the wicked, slays the unjust, and creates so much misery, it seems an unchristian work and entirely contrary to Christian love; but if I think of how it protects the good and keeps and preserves house and home, wife and child, property and honor and peace, then it appears how precious and godly this work is, and I observe that it cuts off a leg or a hand, so that the whole body may not perish. For if the sword were not on guard to preserve peace, everything in the world must go to ruin because of lack of peace." Luther preserves a unity of motive in the Christian life in spite of the diversity of roles, and he sees life as a whole under the same divine rule. He stresses the obligation of the Christian citizen to obey the ruler for the sake of order in matters of war and peace, unless he "knows for sure" that the ruler is wrong. In practice, this leaving moral decisions, in all but

the most extreme cases, to the ruler may create a deep split in
the person between the Christian and the political roles. Luther
had little confidence in princes as persons, but he overstressed
their claims as representing order. His view of war has little in
common with modern warfare, and his assumption as to who is
wicked is strangely one-sided. However, the use of military force
under modern conditions can only be justified, as Luther justifies
it, as the means of preventing the greater evil: "The small lack
of peace, called war, or the sword, must set a check upon this
universal, world-wide lack of peace, before which no one can
stand." But Luther becomes repellent when he says: "For the
hand that wields this sword and slays with it is then no more
man's hand, but God's, and it is not man, but God, who hangs,
tortures, beheads, slays and fights." Luther gives too little attention to the extent to which those who fight to restrain evil become
themselves instruments of evil.[1]

There is great emphasis today in Christian theology on the
affirmation of the secular world. This is one way of insisting on
interaction rather than separation. It is inspired in part by a
sense of responsibility for people beyond all the barriers that
Christians have often set up. It is inspired in part by respect
for the secular interests and institutions on their own terms given
in God's creation and not to be manipulated in external or
heteronomous ways by churches or theologians. Perhaps the
affirmation of the secular that has most meaning for international
relations and foreign policy today is the belief that God is at work
positively (and not only in judgment) in the rising of the neglected
peoples in their struggle for justice and dignity. The tidy, white,

[1] I have received the following comment on this passage from John Raines,
who has lived much with Luther's social ethics. He writes: "One of the
reasons for this was probably his one-sided and negative view of the state
as 'a result of sin and a dike against sin.' This tended to confine his political
ethics within an overly punitive and coercive frame, closing him off from a
more creative exploration of the positive and humanizing functions of the
state. When talking about education, economics or social welfare, however,
Luther was less cramped, and could express more directly the high value he
placed upon secular vocations and God's activity within them." There is always something more to say about Luther.

Western world, which happens also to be the world that has been Christendom, feels threatened by the tumultuous events connected with revolution. The positive attitude toward revolution as the locus of divine action will be discussed in later chapters, but it makes a difference whether our first word is the "yes" of acceptance to the necessity of revolutionary change or the "no" of timid fear for the *status quo* from which the writer and most readers of this book profit.

This positive attitude toward the secular has been needed, but there is one great danger in it: Christians may lose the assurance that there is a distinctive word to the secular, both a positive and a negative word, that comes from the revelation of God in Christ, a word needed also by the "religious." Churches are institutions through which what I call the Christian community speaks and acts and preserves what has been given to it. All that has been given to the Christian community should not be blurred by a refusal to affirm its distinctiveness over against the world. There is no reason for the Christian community, in spite of all its own sins and distortions, to lose its identity as the bearer of the sources of its own correction; and I doubt if the secular world has sources of correction that can take the place of those that come through God's revelation in Christ. Its established institutions are usually, in part, vehicles of injustice. Its revolutions lend themselves to corruption from dehumanizing hatred and fanaticism and idolatry. Those who affirm the secular are right: God works in ways uncharted by the church or by Christian theology, and in the secular world there are sources of correction to which Christians need to be open; but for Christians the ultimate criterion for change is revealed in Christ. Through him comes the understanding of the human and of God's creation and the mediation of the redemption to which it is the duty and the privilege of Christians to bear witness. In this chapter, I shall try to spell out briefly what these are and how they are relevant to international relations. Where there are in the world other sources of understanding and of redemption, I am grateful for them.

What follows in this chapter cannot be learned by listening to the world apart from what has been received from revelation, though I believe there are pointers to it and confirmations of it in the world. It may be rejected as false; but, if it is true, it is most relevant to foreign policy and international relations.

In general, we may say that Christian faith and ethics offer ultimate perspectives, broad criteria, motives, inspirations, sensitivities, warnings, moral limits rather than directives for policies and decisions. These contributions should be spelled out and become part of the mind of the church, not in general terms, but as related to the decisions of citizens in the sphere of foreign policy. Now I shall outline the content of this distinctively Christian perspective.

1. *All nations live under the providence, the judgment, and the love of God.* It is well to be reminded, when we are full of the sense of the greatness of nations, of such words as these: "Behold the nations are like a drop from the bucket, and are accounted as the dust on the scales." "It is he who sits above the circle of the earth, and its inhabitants are like grasshoppers; who stretches out the heavens like a curtain, and spreads them out like a tent to dwell in; who brings princes to nought, and makes the rulers of the earth as nothing." (Isaiah 40:15, 22-23) In the Old Testament, this is the backdrop for affirmations of the coming redemption of the nations; it is only the beginning of any Christian statement of God's rule in the world, but it is a good corrective for the "illusion of American omnipotence." We cannot deduce any rules of behavior from the fact of the finiteness of the greatest nations, but a feeling for this should come upon us when our nation is tempted to arrange the destinies of other nations according to its own prescriptions, without really understanding what is below the surface in them.

The word *God* does not refer to a vague Almighty before whom we are finite creatures. If that were all, it would not be too difficult to convince ourselves that a provident Almighty was on our side. An unrevealed God can be made over in one's own image. But God revealed in Christ, who acted in Christ for the redemption of the whole world, who wills the welfare of each nation as part of the world that he loves, who transcends all nations in such a way that he keeps all their ideals and achievements and ideologies under judgment—God so understood is the ultimate perspective from which we should view our own nation among the nations.

Transcendence and love—to associate these is not based upon some common-sense judgment to which the secular world naturally comes. The transcendence of God over the nation can deliver the citizen from national idolatry, even though the greatness of the nation and the resources of the state so easily surround the citizen with what seems a garment of righteousness. It is difficult for the citizen to be free in his own conscience, unless he sees nation and state under transcendent judgment. As I shall suggest later, we are helped to be aware of this judgment when we consciously live as members of the universal church.

There is always the possibility for an individual to maintain his own freedom of mind through a studied skepticism, but, if this becomes the general outlook of a people, there is always the danger that it will create a spiritual vacuum ready to be filled by a false absolute. Pure relativism does have a critical role, but it is no adequate intellectual and spiritual diet. A provisional relativism in the presence of transcendent love is quite different, for such love does provide ultimate guidance. At least we learn from it what C. H. Dodd finds in the teachings of Jesus: "the obligation to reproduce in human action the quality and direction of the act of God by which we are saved." [2]

2. *The second element in the Christian perspective is the commandment of love.* This is more than a commandment, because it stems from the demonstration of God's love for all men, of which our love at its best is a reflection.

What has love to do with the hard decisions governments make in defending their interests, in deciding what kinds of force to have and when to use them? The Christian citizen lives under the command of God in Christ to seek the welfare of all his neighbors near and far. Concern for the nearer neighbors is the substance of patriotism and has its proper place in the Christian life. Christian love in the hearts of citizens can be translated into terms

[2] *Gospel and Law,* Columbia University Press, 1951, p. 71.

of such generally recognized values as justice and order and peace and freedom. As I have suggested, we experience our chief moral perplexity when these conflict with one another, and we see the depth of this perplexity when some neighbors who are loved of God attack or oppress other neighbors who are also loved of God.

Such conflicts of values give great support to the tendency to claim that there are no general laws, that Christians need only to be guided by what they believe love demands in each situation. *Love God and your neighbor and do what comes to you to do in the moment* is what this doctrine implies.

Certainly we cannot derive from Christian love a series of rules that prescribe their own application to all situations. But I do not believe that an ethic that is purely situational, even if it is under the overall guidance of love, is sufficient. This emphasis on the situation is in many Christian circles the fashion, and it comes from a sound rebellion against a too rigid legalism and also from the deep perplexities that arise when our rules are in conflict. The "New Morality," which plays down all rules, even all general considerations, whether in the area of sex or in the area of international relations, reflects this rebellion.

What is missing in this emphasis upon the situation is that an ethic having no other source of guidance than love and knowledge of the situation has no protection against one's being captured by the situation where it is experienced with great intensity. It becomes far too easy to forget the continuing claims of values and goals which we may sacrifice—even for the sake of love, as it seems—amidst the urgencies and dilemmas of the situation. If we sacrifice the peace for someone's freedom, we should not forget limits to the use of force. If we find ourselves opposed to one group of nations as adversaries in order to defend the freedom of choice of another group of nations, we should not lose sight of the humanity of both groups of nations. Indeed, some of the chief representatives of a situationalist ethic make much of the concept of "humanization." This becomes the great Christian goal, the one source of criteria. But as soon as we look at this concept we see that it does include many criteria. Much must be known about the human normatively and much must be known about the conditions for the realization of the human descriptively satisfying many advocates of an ethic of principles.[3]

Instead of announcing clear-cut moral laws that have applications that can be predicted in advance, we might speak of moral pressures that remain in force in all situations. Even when one such moral pressure may seem to have priority at a given moment in history because of the exigencies of a particular situation, the others should still be strongly felt. There are pressures now upon Christians in this country to preserve an open world in which nations may choose their own social systems, in which there can be much freedom and diversity. At the same time we need to remain under pressure from the revolutionary demands of a part of the world that remains hungry. Christians at a given time may find they are forced to make choices remote from anything they could contemplate as abstractly good or consistent with all the goals and principles to which they are accustomed; but if this happens, let them not forget what they may sacrifice or neglect for the time being. And let the church in its teaching and liturgy be a source of perpetual reminders of all that is involved in Christian faith and ethics.

I have been helped by the findings of Dr. Robert Batchelder in his study of the process of decision that led to the use of the atomic bombs on Japan. He writes: "In findings such as these, this study has to some extent confirmed the contextual approach to ethics, at least as a description of what actually happens to men when they attempt to make moral principles relevant to the difficult and shifting problems confronting them in the course of

[3] There is a considerable literature on the problem of principles versus the context in ethical decision. Paul Lehmann's *Ethics in a Christian Context* (Harper and Row, 1953) is the most thorough and also most provocative statement of a Christian contextualism. There is a very helpful survey of the current discussion in an article by James M. Gustafson: "Context versus Principles: A Misplaced Debate in Christian Ethics." (Harvard Theological Review, April 1965). I agree that the debate is misplaced in the sense that neither of the two positions is really self-sufficient.

history: a new historical situation does lead to a new and different understanding of previously accepted principles. The recommendation sometimes inferred from this by contextualists is that principles ought not to be held too firmly: the moral life is not merely the imposition of rigid ethical norms upon the richly varying stuff of life. The latter is undoubtedly true—but our findings suggest that the impact of new historical experience upon moral principles is so great that if the principles are held too loosely or too vaguely they may be lost altogether in the press of events. What is required is not only a *new understanding* of moral principles in each new historical situation, but also a new understanding of *moral principles* in each new context. Because the impact of historical experience is so great, a firmer (though not rigid) grasp upon principles is necessary. A firmer grasp upon the basic insight of non-combatant immunity would have mitigated many of the excesses of World War II; and a stronger hold upon the ancient principle of the just cause in warfare might have averted much confusion in the thinking about atomic war in the years 1946-1950." [4] I shall have occasion to deal later with the specific issue of "the just cause in warfare"; in this case, perhaps the reference is to just *means* more than to just *cause*.

The very word *principles* may have a too static sound for many people. But unless the moral pressure to avoid wanton destruction of populations remains active, the apparent demands of the moment can provide excuses for monstrous deeds. The bombing of Hiroshima and Nagasaki had been prepared for by the gradual loss of all restraints in the bombing of populations in Hamburg and Dresden and Tokyo. In the case of the bombing of Hiroshima and Nagasaki, there was not only the violation of ancient principles of humanity; there was something else that came with the new situation: the fateful effect for all time of our setting the example of first use of nuclear bombs without warning.

3. *Christian teaching about human nature.* The first half of this century saw the rediscovery of Christian theological wisdom about human nature, about the limits of man in history. This

[4] *The Irreversible Decision 1930-1950,* Houghton Mifflin, 1961, p. 263.

came as a corrective for the uncritical optimism of much liberal theology during the early decades of the century. To some extent it may have come in the form of an over-correction, but that is how theological thought often develops, one generation over-correcting its predecessors.

Two sides of Christian teaching need always to be kept together. The positive side is the teaching about the image of God as created in man, combined with the teaching about the renewal of that image in the redemptive work of God through Christ. Here we have the Christian charter for the humanity of all men. This is the Christian basis for hope. It is also the basis for openness to the humanity of people on the other side of any conflict as well as on our side. The imperative of love is based upon two indicatives: the indicative of God's love for all men and the indicative concerning the humanity of all men as created and redeemed. It is essential to realize that these things are said on a Christian basis not only about Christians but about all men.

The other aspect of this Christian teaching is the understanding of the finiteness and sin of men, beginning with ourselves. It was the special contribution of Reinhold Niebuhr to open the eyes of a whole generation to the fact that the sinful pride and self-centeredness of men appear under various guises on all levels of human advance, that there is no *secure* progress toward overall solutions of essential human problems. Niebuhr speaks generally of proximate solutions, which help us to live with the problems. There is hope that many particular manifestations of the deeper problems will yield to proximate solutions and that the grace of God may again and again—often in surprising ways—neutralize the sin of men, that the providence of God may overrule the egoism of nations and cause "the wrath of men to praise him."

This Christian realism, as it is often called, has had great influence upon thinking about international relations. There is a generally recognized kinship between Reinhold Niebuhr's theological realism and the political realism of such political thinkers as Hans Morgenthau. Kenneth W. Thompson, in a book on the major trends in thinking about international affairs, gives a very

high place to the influence of Reinhold Niebuhr outside the
sphere of theology among the theorists and practitioners in the
field of foreign policy.[5]

Christian realism helps us to recognize the role of power, sometimes aggressive and malignant power, sometimes power as an
instrument of justice and freedom, always power as a source of
temptation. It helps us to see how limited are the possibilities
that policy-makers confront at a given time. It has convinced a
great many contemporary Christians of errors in pacifism as the
key to international politics, though Niebuhr has always had
great sympathy with the vocational type of pacifism, especially
with that of the Mennonites, which involves at least partial withdrawal from political responsibility and which does not seek to
prescribe political policies for government. Christian realism
warns us against idealistic schemes for controlling history, and
reminds us of the obstacles to the leap into world government.
Niebuhr's article, "The Illusion of World Government," and
similar writings had much to do with the reserve of the churches
in this country in relation to all such schemes and with their
support for the United Nations as a more modest alternative.
Christian realism of this type also warns us against the pride
and self-righteousness of our own nation, against the tendency
to divide the world into zones of good and evil, against ideological
absolutes of all kinds, including those that tempt us in the West.

Christian realism needs to be kept up to date. There has been
a tendency for some of its exponents, together with the secular
exponents of political realism, to use this type of doctrine to
sanction policies because they are tough and free from idealistic
illusions or because they fit the strategic needs of the Western
powers. The mixture of ingredients in a policy that was realistic
in relation to the problem of the 1940s may be unrealistic in the
1960s. Realism today calls for greater emphasis on its own warnings against American ideological fixations, and it also calls for
openness to the changes that have taken place in the Communist
world. This phase of Christian realism came into existence at the

[5] *Political Realism and the Crisis of World Politics,* Princeton University
Press, 1960. Also a John Wiley paperback edition, 1965.

time of the menace of National Socialism, which was primarily a military problem, and there has been a tendency to see all later threats too much in military terms.

One other aspect of Christian teaching about human nature is the balance within it between the claims of the person and the claims of the community. Christian teaching should be the source of correction for all one-sided forms of individualism and collectivism. The person transcends his own community because of his responsibility to the God of all communities. Neither the power of any state nor the pressure to conform within any nation should make the person captive. We find here the Christian basis for the freedom of the person in the civil sphere. Yet Christians are made for love. In the context of the church, they are members of a body; in the context of the wider society, they exist to serve their neighbors through the institutional instruments that are available and effective, including the state. The use of Christian ideas of freedom to baptize absolute economic individualism is a great perversion. It is also a perversion to use Christian ideas of responsibility to support uncritical loyalty to the state. In the current ideological conflicts, Christians may choose to support systems that move too far toward either individualism or collectivism, when they are the only alternatives available, but their lives and the teachings and symbolic actions and polities of their churches should always point beyond all systems. Freedom from being possessed by any ideology in the conflict of ideological systems is an aspect of Christian freedom.[6]

4. *The grace of God that seeks out the sinner and forgives those who turn to him in faith.* It may seem strange to speak of this in the context of international relations, but it has great importance as the second chapter of Christian realism. The doctrine of justification by faith has enabled sensitive Christians to live and act in the world, as it is, without self-deception and without despair. The category of justification may not be the most meaningful to people today, but Christian realism came in the form of the discovery of the theology of the Reformation, especially the

[6] I have dealt with this subject more fully in *Christians and the State,* Charles Scribner's Sons, Chapters IX-XI.

teaching of Luther about the continuation of sin among the redeemed, and of the discovery, in spite of this sin, of forgiveness and hope. One of the greatest books of Christian social ethics of this century, Emil Brunner's *The Divine Imperative,* was based upon the doctrine of justification by grace. Brunner said very little about international affairs as such in that book, but he dealt with the predicament of being forced to make decisions that create deep conflicts of conscience.

He put the matter in these strong words: "We never see the real meaning of 'original sin,' we never see the depth and universality of evil, or what evil really means in the depths common to us all, until we are *obliged* to do something which in itself, is evil; that is, we do not see this clearly until we are obliged to do something in our official capacity—for the sake of order, and therefore for the sake of love—which apart from our 'office,' would be absolutely wrong." [7] This reflects Luther's contrast between roles within the life of the Christian in the world, a contrast that must be affirmed. But always, as I have said, we should stress interaction between roles rather than separation, and always we should avoid the development of two independent moral standards for public and private life. Both Luther and Brunner guard against any such complete ethical dualism but neither is emphatic enough in doing so.

In suggesting that the category of justification may not be the most meaningful, I have in mind Paul Tillich's statement that the "question of a merciful God and the forgiveness of sins," which was primary in the theology of the Reformation, has less meaning for people today than "the question of a reality in which the self-estrangement of our existence is overcome, a reality of reconciliation and reunion, of creativity, meaning and hope." [8]

The gospel of grace has been an essential element of Christian political realism, for it has enabled Christians to face with full

[7] Westminster Press, 1947, p. 227.

[8] *Systematic Theology,* University of Chicago Press, 1951, Volume I, p. 49. The more recent trends in Christian thought and the attitudes attributed to "secular" men confirm this negative judgment, whether or not they would support Tillich's statement of the alternative.

honesty the realities with which they have had to live. It has enabled them to live without escape, without self-deception, and without despair. The Christian has always had to face both the consequences of decisions forced upon him by external realities and the consequences of decisions to which he makes his own sinful contribution, decisions made worse by his own self-serving, his own weak conformism, his own cowardice or irresponsibility. These are in practice all fused together, and it is impossible in detail to chart the lines which separate them. There are compromises and compromises, those that are inherent in the situation because one value must be sacrificed in part to another and those that stem primarily from our own moral failure.

The gospel, as understood by Christian realism, makes it possible to choose when all possible choices stab the conscience. The moral burden of this objective evil is not to be measured by the degree of my personal responsibility and guilt. There is a difference here between the thought of Protestant theologians, such as Reinhold Niebuhr and Emil Brunner, and the characteristic trend of traditional Catholic moral theology, which concentrates on a legalistic limiting of personal guilt in the complex moral burden to which I refer. Protestant thought has been untidy perhaps in invoking the forgiveness of God to cover one's involvement in the whole mess of evil. And yet, when the effort is made to isolate that element which is the result of my own personal guilty choice, there is a tendency to be too complacent about the mess as a whole. St. Augustine said of the waging of "just wars," which a Christian has a duty to fight, that there is a great misery about the whole situation—misery, I assume, that extends beyond the misery of personal guilt. He said: "Let every one, then, who thinks with pain on all of these great evils, so horrible, so ruthless, acknowledge that this is misery. And if anyone either endures or thinks of them without mental pain, this is a more miserable plight still, for he thinks himself happy because he has lost human feeling." [9] I believe we should distinguish between the

[9] *The City of God*, Bk. 19, Chap. 7. In the previous chapter, Augustine speaks of the predicament of the judge who believes, according to the custom of the times, that he must torture a prisoner in order to discover the truth about

forgiveness that covers guilt and the healing that enables a person to live with all of this misery. In detail this is difficult, and this should not lead to a reduction of a sense of responsibility to neutralize or to overcome the broader evil.

There is a dimension of true moral experience in sharing the corporate guilt of one's nation. One of the finest expressions of this was the famous Stuttgart declaration in which, at the end of the Second World War, those Germans who belonged to the Confessing Church and who actually had least personal responsibility for the crimes of the Nazis, accepted responsibility for all that the German nation had done.

I have stirred up several problems and my only purpose is to stress the fact that the gospel of grace does enable Christians to face the realities of history and to assume their responsibility without paralyzing guilt. This is the primary fact. It makes it possible to act and to live after the act without crippling disillusionment.

There is always the likelihood that when such a conviction becomes a received doctrine it will be abused. Dietrich Bonhoeffer, in his *The Cost of Discipleship*, writes with great power about the way in which the very doctrine of justification had come to be a justification of sin rather than of the sinner.[10] So this

---

his guilt or innocence. The punishment of the innocent through torture to discover whether they are innocent by a judge with an intention to be just is described. Then Augustine says: "These numerous and important evils he does not consider sins; for the wise judge does these things, not with any intention of doing harm, but because his ignorance compels him, and because human society claims him as a judge. But though we therefore acquit the judge of malice, we must none the less condemn human life as miserable. And if he is compelled to torture and punish the innocent because his office and his ignorance constrain him, is he a happy as well as a guiltless man? Surely it were proof of more profound considerations and finer feeling were he to recognize the misery of these necessities, and shrink from his own implication in that misery; and had he any piety about him, he would cry to God, 'From my necessities deliver Thou me.'" We may be thankful that judges do not face this same dilemma today, but Augustine's point is clearly an illustration of the moral burden in which one may be involved in spite of one's motive.

[10] Macmillan, 1951, p. 44.

aspect of Christian realism may lead to a premature acceptance of a situation, to complacency in the face of preventable evils. To be guided by the prospect of forgiveness in making decisions may not be too far from sinning that grace may abound. This gospel is not a source of guidance concerning the possibilities, but should help us to live with the possibilities that we find to be beyond alteration. It came as a liberating corrective, but now, when it is repeated, it may need correction so that moral sensitivities are not dulled as we face the choices of our time.

Grace often has two meanings, one as an expression of the forgiving love of God but the other as an enabling influence (not different from the meaning of the Spirit in another context), and in this sense the presence of grace may raise the level of possibilities.

5. *The church as an international fact.* The reality of the church can be much more impressive to Protestants now that they see the larger church in which they believe as including the great Roman Catholic Church, which is both inwardly renewed and in a new way related to us all. Not long ago the Roman Catholic Church seemed very alien to most Protestants, often more a threat than an accepted part of the universal church to which Protestants belonged.

The international aspect of this Christian community has great importance for the Christians in any country as they face the problems of foreign policy. This is especially true in the United States where churches still have considerable strength, where they are in a position to act on public issues, and where they are quite conscious of their relations with churches in other nations. To be a member of a Christian community that has origins and traditions and authorities independent of the nation or the national state makes a difference in the way a Christian is related to his own nation.

It makes even more difference to be aware that this community has units in almost all nations among people whose experience of life is markedly different from one's own, among nations in the Communist world and among nations in the southern and economically underdeveloped part of the world. How can American Christians think in the same way about international problems after they have really been exposed to the way in which the world appears to Christians—representing their neighbors in their nations and not as a Christian bloc—in such different places as Chile, India, Czechoslovakia, the Soviet Union, not to speak of Cuba and China? There is a real difference of outlook on Cold War problems, especially in as near and similar a nation as Canada. Recently I received an invitation to an international meeting in Canada sponsored by the heads of leading universities in eastern Canada. It was striking to me that three nations were named "as the three major ideological centers," and representatives from these centers were invited to come to this conference to interpret the policies of their governments. These centers were the United States, the U.S.S.R., and China. Canada by no means regards herself as neutralist or as being unrelated to what is taken to be the ideology that has its center in the United States, and yet there are differences of nuance between Canada and the United States that stem partly from differences in power and in responsibility. But I have no doubt that these very differences in power and responsibility lend themselves to a greater objectivity on some issues, concerning China and Cuba, for example. Also, in Canada there is no rightist movement, not even a strongly conservative movement, that would clamor for victory in the Cold War. The Conservative party has nothing to do with conservatism in that sense so familiar in this country.

I am not suggesting that everyone else is necessarily right and that American policy is necessarily wrong when it is criticized. We do have responsibilities that go with power, and there are inevitable resentments against our bigness. It is hard for people who have no part in our power to see the world as many of our most conscientious citizens see it. Exposure to them may help us to understand better how our policies appear to people who have different experiences of life from ours, but who are affected by what we do. It may help us to understand the Communist part of the world and the hungry part of the world.

I have participated from time to time in meetings arranged by the World Council of Churches, which included representatives in considerable number from Asia and Africa and Latin America; the world as they see it is vastly different from the world as we see it. Priorities and aspirations and fears are different. Often the chief challenges to citizens of the United States come from Latin America where churchmen share the resentment of their fellow countrymen against the stance of the United States in this hemisphere. Often they resent especially the tendency of American policy-makers to see all Latin American revolutionary movement through the lens of an extreme anti-Communism. These feelings have been intensified by American intervention in the Dominican Republic in 1965.

This exposure enables the American Christian to realize he is a citizen of two cities, and that, while these two cities should not be separated in his own life, the view of the world from the ecumenical city helps to correct his vision as a citizen of his nation.

In addition, this participation in the universal church is a source of hope. Hope is not limited to those who are within the Christian circle. Yet, there is a concentration of the means of grace known to Christians in the community that keeps facing toward the revelation in Christ. In the interaction between this community and the world of nations, churches can be purged of false pretensions and rigidities of thought; but also the effects of redemption mediated by churches can overflow into the life of nations. In the days of Christendom, too much was claimed for this overflow. In the days of the "secular city," the tendency is to claim too little, and to expect too little for what may come to humanity even in its political life, from these Christianly recognized means of grace.

3: The Interests and Power of Nations

THERE ARE important discussions about what constitutes a nation, how much nationhood depends upon common language, common memories, political unity, and territorial integrity. Does the idea of nation have meaning where there is no state through which the nation can act? For the purpose of this book, these questions are marginal, because I am concerned with the behavior of nations as political entities. The fate of the world depends upon the national communities that are unified by political institutions, though these institutions would not be effective if there were no other bonds of unity. Some new national states are precarious, because they are continually undermined by tribal loyalties. Nationality, when it is combined with a distinctive language and perhaps a distinctive religion, can be a divisive factor as a political community within a nation. Even a nation as long established and well disciplined as Canada finds itself threatened by the clash of nationalities. Multilingual India will have difficulty in preserving national unity. There are many nations which combine political unity with enough marks of unity as communities to enable them to assert a national will. A few of them have great power. Others, though externally weak, are still capable of national self-assertion in ways that strangely limit or deflect the power of the greatest states.

It is often said we live in a situation of international anarchy, even of a suppressed Hobbesian war of all against all. The anarchy is far from being complete. It is mitigated by very limited legal restraints in areas in which vital interests are not at stake.[1] It is mitigated by the existence of groups of nations, which

[1] Professor Hans Morgenthau has this to say about the effectiveness of international law governing the routine of international relations as contrasted with the more ambitious projections of law to deal with serious conflicts: "It is also worth mentioning, in view of a widespread misconception in this

limit the sovereignty of the individual nation that belongs to them. It is mitigated by many *de facto* restraints growing out of a degree of respect for the opinion of other nations, by the realization of the remarkable power that lies in the resentments of other nations. This is especially true in the resentments over colonialism. The United States discovers quickly the limits of its power in dealing with its neighbors to the south. Cuba can sting the giant, and Panama can embarrass it.

In the present situation these limits upon the power of the two greatest powers arise in part from the fear of provoking one another and from the fear, which is felt especially in the United States, that the Communist countries will take advantage of the resentments in the vast uncommitted world. The American policy in Vietnam is in some respects restrained, especially in the avoidance of bombing of centers of population in North Vietnam. I hope that this restraint will continue and that under no circumstances will the United States bomb Hanoi. An analysis of the causes of this restrained use of power would emphasize genuine reluctance among the policy-makers to bomb populations, a strong and vocal segment of opinion in the United States that would be wholly opposed to such bombing, a general fear of extending the war with incalculable consequences, a specific fear of Soviet or Chinese retaliation. There is one fundamental reason for restraint that has been expressed by those close to policy-making: the desire to have someone with whom to negotiate. There are particular reasons why this is important in this case; we claim to be serving a genuine Vietnamese interest in fighting the war, and this interest can hardly be served by destroying what is now North Vietnam. But this concern can be generalized. Even conquerors do not want to preside over a wilderness. Unless a nation has lost all common sense, not to speak

---

respect, that during the four hundred years of its existence international law has in most instances been scrupulously observed. When one of its rules was violated, it was, however, not always enforced and, when action to enforce it was actually taken, it was not always effective. Yet to deny that international law exists at all as a system of binding legal rules flies in the face of all the evidence." (*Politics Among the Nations*, Knopf, 1956, p. 251.)

of moral inhibitions, it has some concern for the peace that will follow the war.

This outline of some of the restraints which operate among nations today does not give us a pretty picture of order in place of anarchy. There is partially suppressed anarchy rather than dependable order. All that I want to emphasize is that the power of the most powerful nations is limited by something more than the power of their rivals. There is a germ of something better when these restraints reflect moral inhibitions within the nation that is restrained and when they reflect a nascent world opinion.

Woodrow Wilson had great confidence that democratic nations could be expected to be peaceful, an idea that has had wide currency in liberal circles. This expectation has hardly been vindicated as a general proposition. Indeed in recent years such observers as George Kennan, Walter Lippmann and Herbert Butterfield have called attention to the peculiarly belligerent spirit that develops in democracies. Democratic nations can be whipped up into a frenzy of self-righteous hatred, and governments that might themselves be more circumspect than public opinion can be trapped by the rigidity or the fanaticism of the public. This is all true and important. On the other hand, I wonder if it is not also true that, so long as issues have been kept below the boiling point, there are today opportunities for public opinion within a democracy to respond to public opinion in other nations and that this can be a restraining force. It takes time, though perhaps not time enough, for the varied centers of opinion in a democracy to be overwhelmed.

The sovereign national state with some of the limits upon sovereignty that I have mentioned, limits which at times are strengthened through the United Nations, is the chief factor in the world today. Nationalism, the sentiment of loyalty to the nation, still seems to be the most powerful emotion that drives the world's people, more powerful than ideology, even in the Communist world.

We all know the irrationality and idolatry of much nationalism and its destructiveness when it is wedded to a militaristic chauvinism. On the other hand, it is important to recognize that in many situations nationalism is necessary to overcome a divisive tribalism and to enlist the energies of citizens in the building of national communities. I mention this in order to do justice especially to the constructive role of nationalism in new countries that must emphasize unity and loyal service to the nation.[2]

One can reject nationalism and national sovereignty as absolutes and yet recognize the provisional value of nationalism, as the cement that makes possible the formation of viable communities, and national independence, as a means often of achieving and preserving a desirable human freedom and diversity. Certainly there is no finality about existing nations as the units of self-determination or political freedom.

Whenever we think about the moral issue involved in the behavior of nations, we must come to terms with two major concepts, the concept of national interest and the concept of national power. I shall discuss these in turn. (It would perhaps be easier to teach Christian ethics in a world in which neither existed, but that is not my privilege.)[3]

[2] One of the most significant Christian conferences dealing with the problems of the new nations was held at Thessalonica in Greece in 1959. Its report included an illuminating discussion of the positive role of nationalism. Here is a key passage: "The objectives of many post-independent nationalisms are fourfold: (1) To consolidate national unity achieved through national struggle, and to resist the forces of disintegration in the new nation-state arising from tribal, linguistic, regional, caste, and other separatism. (2) To build political democracy, guaranteeing fundamental rights of the human person and minority groups. (3) To engage in a planned economic and social development of the nation. (4) To achieve recognition of status and make its contribution to the community of nations." The second objective is not so clear today, as many of the new nations have accepted authoritarian political systems.

There is a body of literature, produced by the Christian Institute for the Study of Religion and Society in India, that deals with the role of the Christian in "nation building" and should receive attention. One volume edited by P. D. Devanandan and M. M. Thomas is entitled: *Christian Participation in Nation-Building.*

[3] Since I have been most influenced in this chapter by Niebuhr, Morgenthau, and Kennan, I refer here to an article by Robert C. Good: "The National Interest and Political Realism: Niebuhr's 'Debate' with Morgenthau and

National Interest. Thought about national interest that can be defended in terms of Christian ethics should move between two poles. The first pole is the recognition of the responsibility of government as a trustee for the national interest. A wise government can greatly extend the scope of what is regarded as the national interest, but at the end of the day it must still concern itself about the essential security and welfare of the nation which it represents. If there were a nation of Christians, they could perhaps instruct their government to engage in acts of great national self-sacrifice—but there is no nation of Christians. If there were a nation of pacifists, they might instruct their government to disregard all the usual prudential considerations concerning national security in order to show the way to disarmament or some other peaceful goal—but there is no nation of pacifists.

As we think of this pole, which even those guided by Christian ethics cannot disregard, we should not take too low a view of national interest. The real welfare and the real security of a nation, of x number of people, are part of the welfare and security of humanity; at least this may be so, if they are served with ordinary decency and prudence. Christian ethics has always had a place for the love of nearer neighbors as well as for the love of more distant neighbors. As I have said, patriotism is love for the nearer neighbors. It is a great good, even though it is not the highest or most inclusive good. There is a concreteness about it, involving quite definite responsibilities, that may make it a higher good than love for humanity as an abstraction or service to distant neighbors that is in fact ineffectual. There is a provisional division of labor here that has some importance, even though for the Christian it can be overruled and one may be called to serve the most distant neighbors primarily as concrete human beings. Later I shall stress the fact that national interest can be stretched very far to include the interests of distant neighbors. But in the first instance there is this division of labor, and a government is limited by it.

The other pole is the recognition that no person informed by

Kennan" in *The Journal of Politics,* Vol. 22. This is a most helpful canvassing of the issues.

Christian ethics or any other kind of universal and humane ethics can make national interest supreme in his own life when it comes in conflict with broader human interests. All that I have said about the meaning of membership in the universal church underscores this point. It is difficult for any person to live in sight of these two poles at the same time, but this must normally be our life as citizens, and it must in a special way be the life of those who have governmental responsibility. I say "normally" because there are those Christians who may rightly choose to throw in their lot with another country, as missionaries or in some comparable capacity. Their priorities would be different from those of an American policy-maker or diplomat. There are, indeed, various roles involving identification with the people of another nation for a shorter or longer period. In one sense, members of the Peace Corps go abroad as instruments of American policy; yet, if this were uppermost in their minds or if it precluded real identification with the nation to which they are sent, it would be self-defeating. Indeed, one of the most admirable accomplishments of the Peace Corps has been the surmounting of the difficulties in combining its service to the national interest with the genuine caring of its members for the interests of people in other nations. To have prevented the Peace Corps from being used as a weapon in the Cold War was a remarkable achievement. One example of the independence of the Peace Corps was its role at the time of the American intervention in the Dominican Republic; at one stage, its members were the only Americans welcomed and able to move freely in the rebel zone, and they were very useful in relation to many humanitarian projects.

There are at least four considerations that may help Christian citizens to do justice to these two poles in their daily attitudes and decisions.

1. I have already referred to the flexibility of the varying degrees of inclusiveness in one's understanding of national interest. The essential point is that there are real mutualities of interest between nations. These go far beyond the awareness of governments and peoples. There is a genuine solidarity of humanity, which shines through these realities of mutual interest. There

is the obvious point that today all nations have an interest in peace, indeed in finding ways of safeguarding the security of one another. Also, in the long run all nations have a common interest in a general raising of the standard of living of the people of the world. The United States as a world power knows that it has both of these interests. It even has an interest in the improvement of living conditions in the Communist countries, because this is likely to give them a greater stake in peace and in a stable world.

The United States has a great interest in other countries' finding their way to viable governments. This does not mean the United States, as often seems to be the case, should be opposed to revolutions. It should drop its almost automatic opposition to revolutions that have a leftward orientation. The declarations that seem to set the United States against any revolution in Latin America that may be supported by Communists cannot generally be implemented, and they are wrong when they commit us to the perpetuation of terrible injustice because of fear of Communism. But this country is justified in hoping that revolution will not mean wallowing in anarchy for an indefinite period. We are justified in hoping for reasonable stability within nations as well as in international relations. These are in line with the American national interest. We are right in helping nations find alternatives to Communist revolutions, but this should not mean they should be denied the possibility of revolutionary change in every situation, if no alternative to a Communist revolution is available. I shall say more about the grounds for this statement in the next chapter, in which I deal with the Cold War.

I do not suggest that the rationalistic idea of a complete harmony of real interests is valid. Obviously, ideological conflicts do create apparent conflicts of interest that for the moment are decisive, but these often obscure the reality of mutual interests. That there are deep conflicts of conscious purpose between nations is obvious. There are real conflicts of economic interest between nations, between the advanced industrialized nations that compete for the same markets, between these nations and those producing raw materials. The conflicts under present conditions where one-product nations are involved are often disastrous for the poorer nations. Yet, as far as the United States is concerned, even when there are these particular conflicts of economic interest, there is an overriding national interest in the economic well-being of the very nations with which we may be in competition so far as specific products and markets are concerned. No matter how many such conflicts we may have with Japan, for example, we have this overriding interest in the economic health of that country.

A stubborn conflict of interest among nations is the one between nations that have considerable unoccupied territory and unused resources and those that are greatly overpopulated in relation to their territory and resources. There is no full solution to this problem, though the more favored nations will always be slower and more grudging than they should be in providing opportunities for the hard-pressed people in the over-crowded nations. No government would be justified in letting down all barriers, because the interests of its own country should be guarded. The United States, even when it drops its most offensive, discriminatory, immigration policies, has no intention of allowing itself to be swamped by immigrants. A Labor government in Great Britain has reduced immigration from Commonwealth countries. This is a hard problem with which we shall have to live. And it is one concerning which, in the more favored nations, prudence and generosity will be in conflict, but pressures from the heavily populated nations will continue.

To mention this case of irreconcilable conflict of interest is to highlight by contrast those wide areas in which mutuality of interest exists. These provide a great deal of scope for the most sensitive citizens. Here is the chief basis for foreign economic aid, though I shall make a supplementary suggestion about the basis for such aid later.

A second consideration that should help us to deal with the moral problem of national interest, the problem created by its rightful but limited claims, is the sympathetic understanding that other governments, like one's own, are also trustees for the interests of their nations. I have been led to see the importance of this especially by the writings of Dr. Kenneth Thompson and Sir Harold Nicolson, the British authority on the history of diplomacy. It is a commonplace of prudent diplomacy to accept restraints, when one nation comes up against the clear interest of another, and to work out an accommodation rather than push the other nation to the wall. This is ordinary prudence in the case of any nation interested in peace and stability. It will avoid actions that humiliate other nations or threaten their basic security. Professor Morgenthau introduces this qualification of a policy based upon one's own national interest in the following passage: "We are able to judge other nations as we judge our own and, having judged them in this fashion, we are then capable of pursuing policies that respect the interests of other nations, while protecting and promoting those of our own. Moderation in policy cannot fail to reflect moderation of moral judgment." [4]

This diplomatic restraint presupposes reasonably civilized relations between states. They were disrupted in the heart of Europe by the ruthless pressures and aggressions of the Nazis. They are difficult as between the Communist and non-Communist nations during the Cold War period, though the balance of terror created by the threat of nuclear annihilation did produce a similar external behavior between the two nuclear giants, and they learned to avoid pushing each other to the wall. Face-saving opportunities were provided for each other by both Kennedy and Khrushchev during the Cuban missile crisis. The Soviet Union, for whatever reason, went beyond all prudent restraints in placing the missiles in Cuba. It could also be said that the United States has often shown a quite inadequate appreciation of the Russian and Eastern European fear of the rearmament of Germany. The United States has some understanding of this problem, but its policies seem to the Russians to bring West Germany closer to access to nuclear weapons. And the Soviet government could regard the placing of missiles in Cuba as a delayed reaction to the placing of missiles aimed at her heartland in Turkey and elsewhere. Americans may say that their missiles were placed in a

[4] *Politics Among the Nations*, Knopf, 1956, p. 10.

somewhat different period of history when the fear of Stalinist aggression was a rational fear and that somehow the Russian missiles in Cuba seemed to have been put there with less provocation and in colder blood.

As this debate across the Cold War barriers proceeds, the United States would do well to reflect on how asymmetrical our policies must appear to most of the world. We insist that we will have no ideological opponent based on any country near our shores, whereas we have always based our power close to the boundaries of the Soviet Union and of China. There has been an assumption, whether expressed quite in this way or not, that the Communist nations are evil and have no interests that should be respected, whereas what we do everywhere is done for "freedom" and against Communism and hence justified.

Professor Henry Steele Commager says that the "prolonged struggle with Communism which we sometimes call the Cold War, accentuated our innate sense of superiority. To vast numbers of Americans it justified—and apparently still does justify—resort to almost any weapons or conduct. For years now we have heard, and not from extremists alone, that the struggle between democracy and Communism is the struggle between Light and Darkness, Good and Evil, and that the moral distinction is an absolute one." [5]

Prudence enlightened by a measure of empathy should cause the United States to realize that Communist nations have genuine interests as nations and reasonable fears for their security as nations. There have been restraints in not pushing the Russians or the Chinese to the wall, notably in the conduct of the Korean War and in the avoidance of direct threats against China in the course of American operations in South East Asia. Yet, I believe that in our basic attitudes the asymmetrical tendencies persist. The presence of American power near the borders of China can be no more tolerable to any Chinese government than the presence of Russian power in the Caribbean is to us.

What was a matter of everyday prudence in the relations between states—this allowance for the other nation's interests as

[5] *Saturday Review,* July 10, 1965.

a rightful concern of its government—has to be achieved again in relation to our Cold War adversaries as nations. This will take imagination and the overcoming of our own assurance that the ideological conflict justifies anything that we feel called upon to do against Communist nations. The validity of this position depends upon the kind of reconsideration of the ideological conflict itself that is the subject of the next chapter.

3. I have learned especially from George Kennan and Hans Morgenthau the role of national interest as a limiting concept. Both men have continually criticized moralism in foreign policy from the standpoint of national interest. The first impression is that this appears to sacrifice morality to national interest, but actually it can be the basis of an essentially moral limitation of the use of national power. A nation that uses its power to press its moral ideals on other nations is likely to throw its weight around far too much for its good and theirs.

It is easy for Americans to see this in the case of the Communist nations. Do we not breathe a sigh of relief at any sign that Russia is concerned about its real national interests and is less interested in crusading for Communism? We hope for the day when this may also be true of China.

National interest may cause a nation to extend its empire for the sake of its security or for the sake of its prestige or for the sake of possible or imagined economic benefits; but as long as a nation is guided by a rational sense of national interest, there is some chance of its settling down and accepting limits to its power and its aggrandisement. This may not happen until the nation has had its fling and then has come up against limits that are set by the power of other nations. As long as there is a power vacuum, nations will usually extend themselves. The United States did this in extending itself on this continent in the nineteenth century. There is great truth in the claim that whatever limits the Soviet Union has accepted are the result of the effective defense of the West and other deterrents created by Western power. Most nations that can do so have their fling, and yet it is possible for them to learn lessons from history and to accept limitations the more wisely they view their own interests.

Kennan's criticism of moralism in foreign policy is, in large part, a significantly *moral* call for national limits. He worries about the tendency of moralistic nations to assume they know what is best for everyone else. Such national virtues as humility and tolerance of the ways of other peoples are likely to be more humane in their effects than is positive commitment to ideals that nations seek to make universal by the use of their power. The division of nations between those that are morally good and those that are morally bad is the source of conflicts so deep that compromise and negotiation are difficult, if not impossible. It is more likely to lead to holy wars that will not end until one side has surrendered or has been destroyed.

Morgenthau, in his idea of national interest as limiting the use of national power, describes the result of moral crusading in these words: "What is good for the crusading nation is by definition good for all mankind, and if the rest of mankind refuses to accept such claims to universal recognition, it must be converted by fire and sword." [6] Morgenthau's opposition to the United State's policy in Vietnam comes from his view that it is not in the real interest of this country. He sees it based upon illusions concerning the degree of the national substance to be defended in South Vietnam, upon illusions generated by the American ideological opposition to all forms of Communism.

There are many facets to Morgenthau's thought, and the limitation of American action that he emphasizes needs to be seen against the background of the American capability to preserve a preponderance of nuclear power to check the emerging power of China; this needs to be seen against the further background of Morgenthau's belief that the use of nuclear power is utterly irrational. This last position needs to be viewed in the light of his conviction that the inability to use this ultimate power makes the whole system of sovereign states irrational and unable to deal with the problems of the nuclear age. Morgenthau sometimes reveals that he is a moralist at heart. One interesting example of this is an article after the death of Adlai Stevenson in praise of his kind of greatness. It was a greatness that, while

[6] *In Defense of National Interest,* Knopf, 1951, p. 37.

tragically frustrated in some respects, consisted "not in the single-minded pursuit of power but in the ability to subordinate the pursuit of power to transcendent intellectual and moral values." [7]

The upshot of this discussion of national interest as a basis for the limits on the use of power does not mean that national interest should be made the ultimate criterion for a nation or that such a view should be sanctioned by Christian ethics. But it does mean that national interest is a useful guide to action, especially if it produces second thoughts about moral crusading.

4. A fourth consideration that helps us to live with the claims of national interest with moral integrity is suggested by a rather strange passage by George Kennan. He writes: "We should conduct ourselves at all times in such a way as to satisfy our own ideas of morality. But let us do this as a matter of obligation to ourselves and not as a matter of obligation to others." [8] This is Kennan's way of expressing what Robert Good calls his "moral modesty." He is fearful of the pretensions involved in universal moral claims that lead one to assume that he knows what is good for others. I do not believe the statement can stand, for our obligations to others—combined with humility in making judgments about them—is surely a part of "our own ideas of morality" and, in this context, of our obligation to ourselves. But there is a point in what Kennan says. It may mean that it is in line with a full view of the national interest that the people in a nation should be able to live with their own consciences. This may not be very different from Walt Rostow's emphasis on the idea that what our nation does should be consistent with our "national style" as a humane nation.[9] But this humaneness is not merely a matter of taste. It is also a matter of conscience, of conscience formed in the United States in considerable measure by the biblical tradition. This takes us far beyond any tendency to make national interest itself the ultimate criterion of national behavior,

---

[7] *The New Republic*, August 7, 1965.

[8] *Realities of American Foreign Policy*, Princeton University Press, 1954, p. 47.

[9] *The United States in the World Arena*, Harper, 1960, pp. 528 ff.

for it means that it is to our national interest to be able to live up to other norms.

This kind of national morality is often expressed through the announcement that such and such a policy is required by our national honor. If there were ever an ambiguous concept, this whole notion of national honor is one. It is a mixture of what is little more than "face" or "prestige" with some fragmentary notions of moral integrity of the kind that Kennan suggests. It seems to me that, more often than not, what is called national honor lacks any moral significance and is little more than a rhetorical defense of whatever policy a nation chooses. Even when the idea of honor is attached to the keeping of an agreement, this can be a very selective matter. National honor in the moral sense and faithfulness to the pledged word are certainly closely related. One of the problems here is how such faithfulness is to be related to a reasonably prudent understanding of the total human consequences of keeping one's word, especially when conditions have changed since it was pledged and the consequences of action are beyond all that could have been imagined at that time. It may seem cynical to subordinate honor to prudence; but when honor is rigidly understood in a rapidly changing world, it should not be separated from prudence when national action can lead to a common disaster. To vindicate national honor though the heavens fall is the kind of moral rigidity that needs to be tempered by prudence and compassion. Who is sufficient for these moral judgments?

All that I have said about living with one's conscience does not mean that governments should be guided by the private consciences of their leaders to the point where they would sacrifice the nation's chance for survival to satisfy their moral preferences. But there are many sacrifices less than this that may well be in line with a very widespread caring for people in other nations. Senator Fulbright has expressed this very well in a recent discussion of the basis for foreign aid. He criticizes the habit of thinking that the United States should get credit for any aid given, and he shows a remarkable sensitivity for the feelings of other nations at this point. The following passage states the basis in the national conscience for foreign aid as well as it can be stated, in my view: "The continuing need for the rich countries to assist the poor countries is a matter of both political and moral compulsion. It is difficult to see how the world's less developed countries can overcome their enormous social and economic problems without generous assistance from the more favored nations, and it is difficult to see how the rich countries can expect to be secure in their affluence as islands in a global sea of misery. But beyond the social and economic and political and strategic reasons for the rich aiding the poor is the simple motive of humanitarian conscience." [10]

I should avoid emphasis on "generosity," and I think that in this context Senator Fulbright does also, because rich nations should not expect gratitude from aided nations. It is better to stress the mutuality of interests than it is to stress generosity or conscience. And yet the very solidarity of humanity that underlies this mutuality also guides the conscience. I believe there is a pervasive conscience in the United States that is able to put all other positions on the moral defensive in the arena of national debate. If leaders take this line and are able to clear away confusions and meet some of the detailed criticisms of particular foreign aid projects, they have a good chance to get a clear mandate from the public, more easily perhaps than from Congress whose members are afraid of local punishment from organized minorities.

These four considerations may help us to live with the difficult problems created by the claims of national interest on citizens and governments. But we are not likely to see the degree to which there is mutuality of interests among nations nor will we continue to have the pervasive national conscience of a humane nation unless many people, including many leaders in government and agents of government abroad, care in their hearts about much more than national interest, unless they care about what happens to people in other countries. Even to have an enlightened view of national interest on the part of a nation as a whole depends

[10] Senator William Fulbright, *New York Times Magazine*, March 21, 1965.

upon there being within the nation many generous and committed people who see beyond the boundaries of national interest, however it may be defined. The role of the churches is obvious in nourishing this way of feeling and thinking. I am impressed also by the fact that most of our widely respected national leaders have been persons of notably generous spirit in relation to the world as a whole. This has surely been true in recent decades of Franklin and Eleanor Roosevelt, of Herbert Hoover (in spite of the rather narrow ideological stance of his later years), of Eisenhower, of Kennedy, and of Stevenson, to name only a few. I felt the truth of this especially at the time of the death of President Kennedy. Why was the grief so universal outside this country? No one doubted that John Kennedy was devoted to the American national interest, but people in other countries felt that he transcended this and that he cared for their dignity and welfare for their own sake.

Also, there was something else in President Kennedy and in other national leaders of comparable stature: a deep desire for a world community in which all nations may have a better life together. To be able to live in such a community is itself an American national interest; yet I doubt if people will realize what this means if their attention is always focused on American interests.

National Power. National power is a great embarrassment to Christian moralists. But it needs to be accepted as one of the given elements that are basically neutral. While corruption by power is a major form of man's universal sin, we need not be fatalistic about particular degrees of corruption; the art of government is to design ways of arranging power that keep it exposed to criticism and that limit it without producing perpetual stalemates. The limiting of power also depends upon power. Within a well ordered nation, this may be largely disguised, but, in international affairs, the presence of power to check power is out in the open and, unfortunately, the most conspicuous forms of power are the most deadly ones, though these are not the only or necessarily the most effective forms of power, even among the nations.

To see national power in perspective, it is helpful to think in general terms about the nature of power itself. Paul Tillich, who was a master of what is general, defined power as "being actualizing itself over against the threat of non-being." [11] Such a definition should at least help us accept the fact of power and admit its moral neutrality! Closer to ordinary observation of power, we may define it as the capacity to produce intended effects, to modify slightly a definition by Bertrand Russell: "Power may be defined as the production of intended effects." [12] Power, seen in these broad terms, is obviously of many kinds. It may be the power of persuasion, or it may be the power of the most cruel violence and terror. It may be what Bertrand Russell calls "naked power," power that has within it no element of persuasion or even of beguilement. It is sheer coercion of the wills of others. Military power is naked power, though it may be used in combination with persuasion. Hans Morgenthau, whose political realism is known for its emphasis on power, says that "power may comprise anything that establishes and maintains the control of man over man." He goes on to say that "thus power covers all social relationships which serve that end, from physical violence to the most subtle psychological ties by which one mind controls another. Power covers the domination of man by man, both when it is disciplined by moral ends and controlled by constitutional safeguards as in Western democracies, and when it is that untamed and barbaric force which finds its laws in nothing but its own strength and its sole justification in its aggrandizement." [13] There seems to be something missing here. If we think of power as the capacity to produce intended results, this may begin with persuasion that involves a degree of power of man over man, but it may result in a degree of mutuality, which this passage hardly describes; and even though there is a background of potential control of some men over others in preserving the very system of mutuality, the system itself cannot be described only as the power of man over man. However, in the interna-

[11] *Love, Power and Justice,* Oxford University Press, 1954, p. 47.
[12] *Power,* Norton, 1938, p. 35.
[13] *Politics Among the Nations,* Knopf, 1956, p. 8.

tional sphere, such a system of mutuality and consent is rare and tenuous.

The struggles of disadvantaged people for social justice involve the organization and focusing of power. The process may be entirely non-violent, but it does involve the economic power of a strike or a boycott and the political power of popular organizations that produce results in election. Even if, at its center, it is non-violent, it is likely to be accompanied by violence. Throughout the process, there may be the power of persuasion, the winning of support from public opinion, even enlisting consciences on the other side of the conflict. Failing successful persuasion before a change has taken place, it may be accepted in time as a *fait accompli* partly because it is the law, but partly because events may have proved that it is not quite as injurious to them as opponents had feared. Even at best there is the power of the police to force compliance from what may have become a small minority. At each stage, power is exerted. To act politically is to seek power for use in these ways.

When we come to the power of nations, we must begin by emphasizing that the political organ of the nation, the state, is itself the dominant center of power in relation to the internal affairs of the nation. It does not have a monopoly of power, for many organized groups have various kinds of power to influence action by the state or to act for themselves. But in reasonably well organized nations, the state does have in principle a special right to use force. It is an exaggeration to say that states have a legal monopoly of force. The somewhat anachronistic right of the citizen to bear arms abridges the state's monopoly of force, and actually there is lawless force even in the best regulated nations and a vast amount of it in the United States. It is fair to say that by its very nature the state has a predominance of force. The power of the state within a nation is enhanced by the existence of its military establishment, designed primarily to defend the nation against attack from outside. The effect of the military establishment within the nation and its influence on foreign policy is an enormous subject in itself.

The power of a nation in the world of nations is itself varied, but the ingredient of military force, whether or not it is used, is the most obtrusive form of national power. It may be irrelevant to many situations but even then there is a great temptation to use it because it is better understood than the political measures which may be required. Also, we now have the experience of possessing forms of military power that are too destructive to use at all.

One of the realities that makes action by the United States in many parts of the world especially difficult is that we add to our military power the power of our dynamic economy. When a very strong economy touches nations with weak economies, it seems to raise all the threats of neo-colonialism. The disproportionate powers of nations in the economic sphere means that for a long time great responsibility will be attended by many embarrassing and self-defeating factors. This is a given situation with which we shall have to learn to live and which we shall hope to change gradually.

Within the nation, justice and freedom depend upon some balancing of the power of various groups and interests under the rule of law. When there is a single party or clique or interest— one economic class or one region or one linguistic or religious group—that has unchecked power, it tends to override all who have no political or economic power to defend themselves. The phrase "balance of power" as used in the context of international relations points to the necessity of being able to check the arbitrary and oppressive use of power by one nation or one group of nations.

Nothing can take the place of the checking of power by power in any area of life, and this is true of all kinds of power. Often, what is involved may be little more than the power to get interests strongly expressed so that they are not neglected, even, as we know, in quite harmonious families. This checking of power by power need not be war of all against all but rather mutual checking of power under law within an overall community in which common loyalties and friendship, in Aristotle's sense, greatly qualify the use of power.

In the world of nations, the checking of power by power is closer to the Hobbesian picture of war of all against all, though fortunately this is not entirely the case in the world as a whole, and between many nations there are common interests and traditions and a variety of friendly contacts. The concept of balance of power is very ambiguous; and any actual balance of power is precarious, because each nation that has a chance of doing so seeks to upset the balance in its own favor. Indeed, the expression "a favorable balance of power" is sometimes used.

Professor Inis Claude, in his *Power and International Relations,* shows up the ambiguousness of "balance of power" as a concept and suggests that the only common meaning it has is distribution of power.[14] The distribution of power is always unstable. One reason for the fear created by the nuclear arms race is that each side never knows when the other may come to possess that final increment of power that relatively may make all the difference. And, as Professor John G. Stoessinger puts it, in a discussion of the relational nature of power, "when capabilities are equal, as in a stalemate, power tends to disappear altogether." He also makes the important point that actual capabilities do not of themselves determine the power of a nation, for this "may depend in considerable measure on what other nations think it is, or even on what *it thinks* other nations think it is." [15]

Unstable as the distribution of power is, and desirable as it is that it be in a framework of international order in which there is lawful power above the nations, the distribution of power is itself a great good in the interests of justice and freedom.

These are all quite elementary matters that may be obvious to most readers, but I emphasize them because for Christian ethics power has often been such a great stumbling block and I want to have them as background for a few affirmations that are directly related to the main concerns of this book:

Power cannot be wished away.

Power in itself is neutral and can be used for many purposes.

Power is of many kinds, and, even among nations, the military

---

[14] Random House, 1962, Chapter 3.
[15] *The Might of Nations,* Random House, 1961, p. 17.

forms of power, which are so obtrusive, are limited in their efficacy and, indeed, may be self-defeating. Among nations, the power of persuasion, the power of non-cooperation, the power of national resentment which may spread indeterminately—especially in the context of resentment against colonialism—the power of national aspiration can be mighty.

Power does need to be checked by power. To allow a nation or a group of nations to have a monopoly of the decisive forms of power, for example, nuclear power, would be a threat to so many values, that responsibility to prevent this from taking place cannot be lightly discarded.

Power should not be considered static. There will be new constellations of power. The nations that have only recently come on the stage will in time be able to change the configuration of power. Nations now on top of the world should not assume that they have a God-given role of guardian of the *status quo* that is so favorable to themselves.

4: The Cold War and Beyond

IN THIS and the two following chapters, I shall deal with three major issues that confront us daily in the sphere of international relations. I shall write about each of them against the background of Christian presuppositions, but I shall not attempt to spell these out in most cases. These chapters may best be taken as one person's attempt to find his way amidst the complexities which call for decisions now, and yet concerning which there is no definitive Christian guidance. The most one can do is to contribute to the discussion by telling what he sees happening in the world and by affirming some of the moral convictions that seem most relevant to current decisions.

*   *   *   *   *

The Cold War between the Communist and non-Communist nations has been the dominant reality in international relations since about 1947. It has created great fears and has generated deep ideological commitments on both sides. It has been aggravated by the possession of nuclear armaments on both sides, though these have to some extent diverted attention from ideology to the immediate problems of survival. But survival has been the more threatened by the hostilities and the mutual distrust resulting from the Cold War. The planned prevention of ordinary human relations and communications between masses of humanity has itself become an intolerable moral condition. In this chapter, I shall discuss interpretations of events, policies, and attitudes, which at least point beyond the Cold War. I shall write as an American who shares many views prevalent in the United States on the issues of the Cold War but who believes that all Americans should try to free themselves from some ideological positions that became frozen nearly two decades ago.

By ideology I mean nothing that is esoteric or technical, no more than a pattern of ideas with which the nation has become identified, including familiar political and economic ideas, which have become fused with moral commonplaces into a fighting creed that prevents openness to the real situation. Ideology as an American phenomenon probably involves rigidity more than it does the passion often associated with the word. The main purpose of this chapter is to give reasons for criticizing this ideological rigidity, so that Americans can do more than they are now doing to overcome the conflict that we call the Cold War.

I shall begin by stating some basic assumptions that condition all that follows. Some of these may seem to be concessions to the ideologies that I criticize, but ideologies gain much of their strength from elements of truth in them.

1. The United States and its Western allies have been right in their resistance to the spread of Communism by force from country to country. Facing Communism as a world-wide phenomenon, they were right in seeing in it an absolutistic system, first absolutistic in its thought and in its claims and then absolutistic in its political institutions. In its early stages, Communism is a messianism with many illusions, which seeks by its doctrine, by its projected programs that in themselves have merit, by propaganda, and by conspiratorial and revolutionary tactics to extend its influence and power. The capacity of Communism to convince a small, well disciplined, committed, and able minority in so many countries that it had in this absolute way the right understanding of history and society and the key to the future is one of the most extraordinary developments of all time. After Communism gained a base in the Soviet Union and later in China, it had the attraction of these nations and their social experiments, together with their military power and diplomatic influence, as essential aspects of its strength. Here was a weak, revolutionary movement, beginning chiefly as an idea in the minds of a few brilliant and resourceful zealots, coming to command the vast power of these nations. Believers in Communism have been convinced that they were right, that they alone offered humanity its salvation in history, and that any means of gaining

and consolidating power seemed justified. The early stages of Communist rule in country after country meant rule by terror and the attempt to transform the whole culture under the guidance of what was presented as Communist orthodoxy.

One of the most successful and most admirable efforts of the United States in its history was its contribution to the reconstruction of Western Europe after the Second World War and its defense of Europe against the threat of Communist expansion. Compared with American undertakings in Asia that have the same purpose, this defense of the European nations was comparatively simple. These nations were all viable communities with strong traditions of political freedom, and they had gone quite far to solve their social and economic problems. They were immune to Communist infiltration for the most part, because they had used democracy to transform capitalism in the interest of most of the community. They already had some of the good fruits that a Communist revolution promises, especially modernization and the welfare state.

However, there was in Europe a military threat to these nations, perhaps less of a threat of invasion or nuclear attack than people in the West imagined, but certainly there were blackmailing pressures which could have brought one nation at a time into the Soviet orbit. Perhaps, even in the days when such fears were most justified, there was exaggeration of the fear of a centralized Communist Europe run from Moscow. Moscow had difficulty in controlling some nations in its orbit, such as Poland, and it lost control of Yugoslavia. It would have found France and Italy, not to speak of Britain, difficult to digest. And yet there could have been a terrible Stalinist smothering of Europe, whether by direct military attack or not, if there had been no power to offset the Soviet power. Blackmail was made easier by the extraordinarily vulnerable position of West Berlin.

Many of the things I shall say later about new possibilities for humanity would probably not be true, if there had not been successful resistance to Stalinist expansion. Not only did this preserve a wide area of freedom and diverse social and cultural and political energies; it also forced the Russians to look for primarily non-military methods of expansion. No one can quarrel with their right to try to make Communism dominant in the world. I emphasize these things to avoid misunderstanding later when I shall speak quite differently about the Communist countries.

2. A second assumption, which may be more than a kind of internalizing of the first, is that Christians and others who have been interested in progressive causes, in radical economic and social change in Western societies, have been right when they have rejected Communism for themselves as the instrument of such change.

In the United States there was some temptation in the 1930s to accept Communist diagnoses and methods but in quite limited circles. It was an attractive simplification of the situation, and to many it was psychologically satisfying as a substitute for religion. But in the United States, this Communist answer was generally rejected not only by conservatives but also by progressives. There is irony in the fact that top leaders of the American Labor movement in the 1960s are still fighting the battles against Communism that were won in the 1930s in this country, and they are more conservative than the cosmopolitan leaders of business in regard to relations with Communist countries. The red-baiting of the McCarthy era was an absurdity, for it came long after the Communist temptation had ceased to exist.

I have written at length elsewhere about the errors of Communism as an absolute system from the standpoint of Christian faith and theology, and I need not enlarge on them here. I believe that what I have said about Communism in the past was correct then, and that it is correct now so far as the Communist ideology is concerned. However, I used to say that Communism, because of its errors, must be a dead end of oppression for all countries where it is established; this chapter will express a different view.[1]

[1] J. C. Bennett, *Christianity and Communism,* Association Press, 1948. This book reflected the early stage of the Cold War and especially such events as the take-over of Czechoslovakia. In 1960, I revised the book under the title, *Christianity and Communism Today,* and indicated the changes that had come in Communist countries, especially the Soviet Union. Both editions deal chiefly with Communism as a faith and as a system of thought and

3. At no point in the conflict with Communism should Christians and other non-Communists have allowed the Communist rejection of religion and its official atheism to turn that conflict into a holy war between Christians and Communists. The Marxist criticism of religion has been partly justified; it has been a judgment upon the conservatism and social escapism of the Christian churches and especially upon their inadequate response to the industrial revolution. Christian theologians, under the influence of Bonhoeffer's rejection of "religion," are more sympathetic today than they were as recently as a decade ago to the Communist criticism of religion and to the Communist atheism, which was partly the rejection of false conceptions and images of God. There is more truth in Karl Barth's nonchalant approach to Communist atheism than there has been in most Christian polemics. He said we need not think of God as a-human because men may be a-theist.[1] It is true, however, that the idolatry of the Communist scheme as the means of human redemption is a profound and dangerous error, and theoretical atheism is an intellectual protection for it.

To allow any political conflict to become a holy war is to intensify the fury on both sides and to make impossible the resolution of the political differences. Political conflicts in this world must be settled by compromises and accommodations; holy wars or moralistic crusades are difficult to settle in that way. The religious conflicts themselves can only be overcome by relationships rather than by separation, by witnessing in love rather than by hostility; holy wars make such relationships and such witnessing impossible.

---

with the conflict on that level between Christianity and Communism. It is still important to deal with Communism as an ideology in many contexts: the context of Chinese Communism, the context of pre-revolutionary situations such as Latin America, and the context of the rigidities and intellectual timidities and the various blinders in seeing the world that remain in the older Communist countries even when much of the spark of ideological faith has gone.

[1] Karl Barth, *How to Serve God in a Marxist Land,* Association Press, 1959, p. 57. In this book Barth seems to me too nonchalant about issues of religious liberty in Communist countries.

What I am saying here about the rejection of a holy war against Communism is in line with the main Protestant teaching about Communism. It is expressed in many ways in all that has come from the World Council of Churches since its formation, and also it is consistent with the teaching characteristic of the National Council of Churches and the major denominations in the United States. Roman Catholicism has been more inclined to unite the political and the religious conflicts into a holy crusade. However, the Popes have avoided any encouragement of anti-Communist militarism; they have been more circumspect in this respect than much American Catholicism. In recent years a profound change has come over Catholicism because of the influence of Pope John XXIII, who gave many evidences in word and deed that he wanted his church to take a more open attitude toward Communists, in spite of its condemnation of Communism. This change came at an opportune time as far as the political conflicts of this country are concerned; it kept American Catholicism from feeding the anti-Communism of the American rightists. American rightists, who flourish best in Protestant soil though most churches oppose them, are still the chief examples of the holy war psychology in what is claimed to be a Christian context.

4. My fourth assumption is that Americans in 1965 must make more explicit to themselves the distinction between Communism as an absolute system and the many and varied Communist nations. We need to take seriously the fact that nations do not long retain absolute ideological commitments, and we should be open to the human changes that take place in Communist countries with the passing of the generations and the lessons learned in spite of ideology from historical experience.

Again we may be very thankful for the influence of Pope John XXIII. As I have said, his church was inclined to deduce its anti-Communism as a philosophical and theological response to the ideology, beginning with its materialism and its atheism. Pope John opened the door to a new approach by many a gesture, not least by his stance in Italian politics with its "opening toward the left." One of the most significant evidences of this new attitude was the fact that the Vatican Council was never used as a sounding board for tirades against Communism, something that could have been expected in the light of the usual Roman Catholic position on the subject. At its final session, less than a third of the bishops at the Council voted for an explict condemnation of Communism. I have in mind also the famous paragraph in *Pacem in Terris* in which the Pope made the precise distinction I am emphasizing here; he does so, though, in general terms and does not mention Communism or Communist nations. In this paragraph (159), he distinguished between the original philosophical inspiration of political movements and the way in which such movements have developed. He says: "It must be borne in mind furthermore, that neither can false philosophical teachings regarding the nature, origin and destiny of the universe and of man be identified with historical movements that have economic, social, cultural or political ends, not even when these movements have originated from those teachings and still draw inspiration therefrom. Because the teachings, once they are drawn up and defined, remain always the same, while the movements, working on historical situations in constant evolution, cannot but be influenced by these latter and cannot avoid, therefore, being subject to changes even of a profound nature." The Pope's attitude toward the Eastern countries at the time this encyclical was published makes it natural to assume that he had in mind Communism as well as democratic forms of Marxism and the nineteenth-century Liberalism that were the targets of his predecessors.

5. My final presupposition is that in that part of the world where revolutionary change is most needed and where Communist ideology as an absolutistic revolutionary creed still attracts many of the most ardent and sensitive advocates of revolution, the main responsibility of Western Christians and of American citizens working through their government is to seek to help nations find forms and instruments of revolution that are more favorable than Communism to the development of an open society, but that at all costs they should avoid an anti-revolutionary or counter-revolutionary stance. Sometimes the alternatives will be very grim, and it will be impossible to have any one policy for the many diverse situations.

It is especially important in this context to overcome the common tendency to look first for military solutions of problems. Military defense against Hitlerism was primary. Military defense in Europe against Stalinism was very important, because Stalinism had little chance to win over the countries of Western Europe by encouraging internal revolutions. As I have said, they already had many of the fruits of revolution, because they had become modernized, and they had semi-Socialist, semi-capitalist economies that had been responsive to the needs of the industrial workers. But in Asia, Africa, and Latin America, the real power of Communism comes from the vulnerability of the societies to the revolutionary appeal of Communism and not primarily because of its military force. Military measures as holding operations may sometimes have a place, but they are subordinate to constructive efforts to develop alternative forms of revolution. Later I shall have more to say about whether or not we should always regard the stopping of Communist advance as a Christian or as an American obligation. The very size of our military establishment makes it difficult to grasp how irrelevant it is to many situations.

It may seem unnecessary to say it, but it should be made clear that opposition to Communism should not be allowed to become opposition to a socialistic organization of society. The American ideological identification with capitalism may often handicap us as a nation in helping another nation that needs radical change find an alternative to Communism. The famous Clay report on foreign aid, which advocated discrimination against socialistic projects, and the Congressional vote against support for an Indian steel mill that was to be operated by the government are indications of this ideological bias. We need to be more pragmatic here and willing to accept the greatest variety of combinations of public and private initiatives. The Communist nations are becoming more flexible themselves, and in our own national life the welfare state is being accepted in practice on a large scale, even though the ideological inhibitions remain.

I have prepared the way to deal directly with the main subject of this chapter: the possibility of moving beyond the Cold War.

Professor Z. Brzezinski in his book, *Alternative to Partition*, makes the startling statement that "the cold war in Europe has lost its meaning." [2] A few paragraphs later he refers to the "emerging post-cold war conditions." Such statements are startling because they come from one of the chief academic authorities on Eastern Europe, who has generally followed a rather "hard line" in relation to Cold War policies. Actually he has had a dual approach emphasizing both military containment and deterrence at considerable risk and yet taking seriously the changes in the European Communist world that were in his judgment encouraged by the hard military line, which proved to the Russians that they must accept co-existence. In this book, he promises no secure solutions to the problems that have created the Cold War, especially the German problem, but he accepts the fact of change behind the Iron Curtain, and he sees possibilities of overcoming the division of Europe that would have seemed incredible ten years ago.

It is my fear that American attitudes formed by the Cold War have been so largely frozen that it will be difficult for us as a nation to respond creatively to the changes that are coming fast. I am not referring primarily to the administration (at least, in regard to Europe) but to large sectors of public opinion still reflected in Congress. President Kennedy gave a signal for the beginning of a change in the American outlook in his American University address in June 1963. He called for a re-examination of the American attitudes toward peace, the Soviet Union, and the Cold War. When had an American president called for changes in American attitudes toward the Soviet Union, instead of changes only in the attitudes of the Soviet Union toward the United States?

The American response to Chinese Communism, which is now in its early and fanatical stage and which must be seen in the context of the fantastic potential strength of China as a nation, is the most baffling problem of foreign policy in this decade.

I shall now outline two changes, related to the Cold War, that

[2] McGraw-Hill, 1965, p. vii.

have taken place in the world and should now be guides to policy. They should be seen as signs of hope.

These two changes are (1) the diminishing of a global unified Communist threat to what we call the free world and (2) the gradual humanization of the Communist countries in Europe. Neither of these changes in itself is a promise that any Communist nation will adopt a policy or a strategy that is favorable to American purposes or to the overcoming of international tensions. These may come and go and then come again. But these two changes have enormous importance for thinking about policy, about what is at stake in the present world conflicts, and they do provide hope that humanity will survive the Cold War and, at least, have a new chance to find the way to peace.

The diminishing of a global, unified Communist threat to the "free world." One can realize the significance of this change only if one remembers the fears that plagued Americans only a few years ago. We saw the unified Communist world increasing in size and power, and we saw the non-Communist world decreasing in size and power. It looked as though time was on the side of that other, threatening world. This naturally created in this country a deep anxiety. It gave to American anti-Communism great intensity and even added to it an element of panic in many circles. The most sober observer of events could not avoid considerable worry about the future of free or open societies.

The split between the Soviet Union and Communist China is the most important fact indicating that the monolith is broken. This split between these two Communist giants has many sources. They are at different stages of development. The Soviet Union is becoming rapidly a more conservative society with an obvious stake in peace. It has too much to lose if it adopts a reckless foreign policy. It has learned more than the Chinese have learned about the nature of nuclear war, though the study by Dr. Morton Halperin, entitled *China and the Bomb*, shows that the Chinese are less reckless than many of us assumed a few years ago.[3] Also,

[3] Praeger, 1965, p. 26. Dr. Halperin writes from the standpoint of American political realism, but he comes to the conclusion that "the Chinese development of an atomic capability is related primarily to defensive objectives—to

there is a long history of antagonism between old Russia and old China that is not forgotten. When people in either nation reflect on their thousands of miles of common boundary, this history comes alive. Any nation, with open spaces, that lives next to a population of 700,000,000 has cause for anxiety. The insults that are traded between these two countries and the ideological battles between their parties are symbols of deep conflicts which are not likely to be overcome in such a way as to make the land mass of Russia and China the home of a unified threat against the non-Communist world. (American policy could conceivably drive these giants together again.) The fact that in the short-run the Soviet Union may feel obliged to play up to the uncommitted world and to the remainder of the Communist world by aggressive talk and even by provocative action in competition with China for leadership is probably much less important than this disappearance of the monolithic threat coming from the East and the West at the same time.

The diversity that is appearing within European Communism is less dramatic than the Sino-Soviet split, but it also reduces what was believed to be the Communist threat. The world of satellites has been broken. This does not mean that in foreign policy these nations may not often vote together and use the same slogans. But this is a concession to the Soviet Union that does not affect their internal freedom. Tito in Yugoslavia was, of course, the first to show that the monolith could be broken. Now the fact that he is more friendly to the Soviet Union is not a sign of greater subservience but rather evidence of a general loosening up of the Soviet bloc. Today there is a spectrum, so far as the development of internal institutions is concerned, with such countries as Yugoslavia, Poland, Czechoslovakia, and Hungary at the more liberal end and with East Germany and Bulgaria at the more Stalinist end. The liberalization within Hungary is against all expectation of a few years ago. Rumania is in a special class, because it has attained more freedom of movement in its relations with other nations than its Communist neighbors and yet at home

---

power status and subtle threats—rather than to specific plans to expand by the use of nuclear force."

it has less cultural freedom than some of them. On this spectrum the Soviet Union would be near the center.

Not only is there diversity among the nations with Communist regimes, there is also a similar diversity among the Communist parties in European non-Communist countries. The independence of the Italian party, the largest of all, has been notable.

Americans might honor these Eastern European countries more if they renounced Communism but, if they did that, they would have less influence on the Communist bloc as a whole. Indeed, it is the contagious relativism that has appeared within the Communist world itself that does a great deal to change the whole climate in that world. If these changes to which I have referred have done nothing else, they have at least had the effect of "relativizing" the absolute doctrine, to quote Professor Brzezinski again.[4]

One possibility that has emerged may in the future affect the American attitude toward Communist movements in Latin America or in other pre-revolutionary situations: a new Communist nation may have a chance to choose between types of Communism. It can play one Communist camp off against another. We need fear it less as a base for international Communism. Indeed, there are many cautious observers who are inclined to believe that North Vietnam, with or without unification with South Vietnam, may be able to maintain a considerable independence of China, if its stamina is not too much weakened by the prolongation of the war in which the United States is involved. Its history is one of resistance to Chinese domination, and the diversity within the Communist world may favor the continuation of that resistance.

The gradual humanization of European Communist nations. I have taken the word *humanization* from a statement by Senator William Fulbright about European Communism. He said: "The Communism of Eastern Europe and the Soviet Union is slowly but steadily being humanized. The terror of Stalin's time has largely disappeared from Russia. The Hungarian government now tolerates a degree of individual liberty. Rumania practices

[4] *Foreign Affairs,* April 1963, pp. 514-15.

a defiantly independent national Communism. Yugoslavia seems slowly and hesitatingly to be coming to accept the legitimacy of doubt about Communism itself." [5]

I quote Senator Fulbright because, while similar things have been said many times by scholars and journalists, I have never seen a statement by a political leader, dependent upon American votes, that has gone so far in admitting the reality of favorable change in the Communist world.

The word *humanization* is better than "liberalized" or "democratized," because these words might cause false expectations of changes that suggest familiar American stereotypes of a free society. There is a tendency in the United States to note what are believed to be changes in the direction of democracy and then immediately to apply a democratic yardstick to these nations, using this as a basis for a continuation of our old criticisms. Neither Russia nor the former European satellites have anything resembling a democratic government. All are authoritarian states, run by Communist parties that are powerful and disciplined minorities. Yet what a remarkable development the humanizing process is: the movement away from government by terror; the growing preoccupation with real social advances from which the people benefit; the beginnings, only the beginnings of cultural freedom; also the growth of "socialist legality," which provides some protection by the courts for the rights of citizens.[6] The very fact of diversity within the bloc is itself a factor that encourages freedom.

There is a fascinating drama taking place in most of these countries: the continual tug of war between the intellectuals on the one hand and the state or party on the other. Poets and

[5] *The New York Times,* May 12, 1965.

[6] George Feifer, an American student of criminal law, has published an account of a year's visits to law courts in Moscow. He gives a fascinating picture of many trials as human events. He gained a respect for the growth of law as touching ordinary crimes, and makes this generalization: "The present Soviet leadership seemed to have learned that legality is far more effective than arbitrariness in cultivating a loyal citizenry and in running an efficient society, and that a stable legal order is a *sine qua non* in a complex industrial society." *Justice in Moscow,* Simon & Schuster, 1964, p. 19.

artists and scientists are expressing themselves with some independence. They take freedom to protest against the forces of oppression and dehumanization. They are partly suppressed, and then they return to fight again. They do not win total victories, but they are not defeated. This is the beginning of freedom. I wonder sometimes why there is not greater interest in this country in this drama. Maybe the intensity of American anti-Communism makes it difficult to believe that the struggle is real. It may be because these Communist intellectuals remain Communists and supporters of their governments in the international arena, and do not say all that Americans want to hear.

It is tragic that in the Soviet Union there is less freedom for the church than there is for the intellectuals. Indeed, in recent years, the church has lost rather than gained, so far as the education of youth is concerned, in spite of its greater economic prosperity and its new ecumenical connections.[7] Perhaps one reason for this is that the intellectuals are respected in a Marxist culture and they have bargaining power, whereas religious institutions are discredited and it is easier to push them around. Ideological defensiveness remains, and freedom to witness publicly to a view of man and the world as different as Christian faith will come hard. But if the cultural freedom grows, religious freedom is likely to grow also. In Poland and Czechoslovakia, there is more religious freedom. In Poland, the church has been too powerful to suppress, even though it has had a continuous struggle. In Czechoslovakia, there is real dialogue between the younger generation of Christians and the younger generation of Marxists. Professor Harvey Cox says that "few of the young Marxist intellectuals I met [in Czechoslovakia] thought of Christianity as trivial or irrelevant. In fact, interest in theology, in some places, particularly in Prague, almost approached the fad stage." [8]

The Jewish community in the Soviet Union is still a special object of persecution. Traditional Russian anti-Semitism, which re-

[7] There has been some improvement since the fall of Khrushchev, but it is too early to know how stable this is.

[8] *The Correspondent*, Winter 1965, pp. 33-34. See also article by Cox, "New Phase in the Marxist-Christian Encounter," *Christianity and Crisis*, Nov. 1, 1965.

appeared in later Stalinism in spite of the role of the Jews in Communist history, is still active though disavowed. It is difficult to know the relation between traditional factors and either the Soviet fear of a religious and cultural minority with such strong Western connections or the Soviet attempt to win friends in the Arab world. At times, outside pressures in behalf of the Jews are followed by minor concessions and, at times, there are literary attacks in Russia on anti-Semitism. Whatever the causes, the Jews are among those who have benefited least from the recent liberalizing tendencies. Pressure from outside, especially as a Christian responsibility, is important and should have considerable effect, if, in other respects, the society continues to become less oppressive. Some advantage can be taken of traditional Communist sensitivity about being accused of anti-Semitism.

Harrison Salisbury is one of the American journalists who are best able to interpret the changes in the Soviet Union. In a recent article, he summed up the consequences of the work of Khrushchev in these words: "Today, when we reckon up the consequences of Khrushchev's act, we find that it has produced: a polycentric Communist world in which such movements as the Italian and the Rumanian are consciously seeking to evolve a form of government and ideology which is based, not on dictatorship of the mind but upon a live-and-let-live relationship that even includes friendship between church and Communist state; the unyielding Russian-Chinese split, marked by polemics, border clashes and a widening network of rival Communist movements, particularly in Asia and Africa; and an urgent and consistent drive within the Soviet Union toward a social system derived from principles and ideals shared with the West."[9]

I can already hear one major criticism of all that I have said about changes in the Communist world. It will be said that these changes do not mean that Communists have really changed their objective; they have only changed their tactics to confuse their opponents. My answer to that criticism is we cannot expect any great historical movement to announce a basic change of objectives. What happens is that changes take place in them often in

[9] *New York Times Magazine,* April 25, 1965.

spite of the conscious purposes of their leaders. The important question today is: what do the Communist nations regard as their real priorities? Priorities may change, while announced objectives remain the same, but this may make all the difference in practice. President Grayson Kirk of Columbia University, who is a careful interpreter of events, says: "Human nature being what it is, it is not to be expected that the Soviet leaders ever would make a dramatic renunciation of past beliefs and practices. Hence, one cannot take seriously occasional American statements to the effect that because the Soviet record is one of duplicity in international dealings, we must avoid placing any trust in any Soviet action unless the Soviet leaders openly disavow their past and announce that they now wish to settle down and become normal members of the world community. This is merely childish thinking." [10] The passing of generations, the erosion of fanaticism, and the natural preoccupation with the improvement of their own societies rather than with world revolution bring about the changes in spite of the ideology, but we cannot expect them to renounce the ideology. They will manipulate their ideology to preserve as much continuity as possible. There is a parallel in the way in which churches change. Often, they change convictions without formally renouncing views to which they were previously committed. And their theologians usually find ways of preserving continuity with the past through re-interpretation.

I happened to see three items in the same edition of the same newspaper, *The Washington Post* of July 14, 1965. One was a sentence in a column by Marquis Childs who is far from being belligerent in his attitude toward Communist nations. He said: "Communism has an inexorable goal with no date set." Such a statement is part of the American ritual. Elsewhere in that paper, there was an article from Moscow by S. S. Rosenfeld about the fact that Russian leaders are worried about the younger generation, which does not share the self-sacrificing zeal of their fathers for the building of Communism and is too cool to the slogans. Perhaps coolness to slogans on our side can keep pace with the same process on the other side. The third item was a statement in

[10] *Foreign Affairs,* Oct. 1964, p. 6.

the financial section by J. A. Livingston about the passing of *Homo Sovieticus* and the tendency of Soviet men to become like other economic men, indeed like Americans, in their goals.

I shall gather together some of the implications of these two changes, changes which are now a matter of our actual experience.

1. The clearest implication to me is that what is at stake in the Cold War has changed slowly, though this is seldom made explicit. In the early stages of the Cold War, Americans saw the world divided into two parts, and that other part was called "the slave world," which seemed condemned to a permanent Stalinist condition. It was often said that Communists "play for keeps," and it was assumed that anywhere in the world, where they might win, their victory would mean slavery for keeps. Now, it is possible to look upon Communism as to some extent open-ended and having the possibility of becoming a constructive experiment after the hard period of revolutionary terror. Remember I am not promising that these internal changes in the Communist world will necessarily produce foreign policies and strategies that are favorable to us, though Russian realism about nuclear war and the necessity of avoiding it is part of the internal change in the Soviet Union.

To realize that what is at stake in the Cold War is not a threat of permanent slavery does not of itself provide guidance for immediate policy, for conflicts of national power will remain, and these can be grave, even if they are about something less than the ultimate fate of men in history. However, something of the fear and of the panic should go out of the Cold War. This has bearing on the old "red or dead" contrast. We want no people to be either red or dead, but we should be careful about asking any nation to risk annihilation when the alternative is not permanent slavery, and we should avoid policies that bring the risk of annihilation to hundreds of millions of people who never had a chance to make the choice. Red is not even one color; there are many shades of color ranging from Chinese red to Polish or Yugoslav red. Already there has been a change of rhetoric in this country, and we hear little about the free world versus the slave world or about the contrast between global annihilation and global tyranny. And yet so far there has been very little explicitness about our realization that what is at stake in the Cold War has changed.

There is an interesting suggestion of how far many of us are from realizing the meaning of what is happening in the very sophisticated book by Dr. Morton Halperin *China and the Bomb,* to which I have referred. The author makes a good deal of the point that the split between Russia and China creates a problem for the United States: the problem is that we shall have to accept the ambiguity of the Cold War.[11] He says that a situation in which the United States and Russia agree in opposing Chinese aggression in Asia (against India, for example) "would complicate the moral issues of the cold war and undoubtedly create difficulties in the American Congress and among certain sectors of American public opinion; more important, it would significantly enhance Soviet prestige in Asia." [12] I am interested in the words, "would complicate the moral issues of the cold war." The main purpose of this chapter is to make a contribution to the complicating of the moral issues of the Cold War.

2. The fact that Communism has proved to be more openended than once seemed possible should mean that our attitude toward nations in which Communism is now established should become sympathetic rather than hostile, so far as their internal affairs are concerned. The deep hostility against Communism as such has made it difficult to take such an attitude toward any of these countries. I was struck by the unusual character of an editorial about Russia in the *Commonweal* in April 1964. It went so far as to say: "Communism within Russia should be looked upon as an experiment that deserves a chance to succeed." [13] That encouraged me, because it came from a greatly respected Roman Catholic journal. I believe that the actual American policy in relation to the Soviet Union is based upon that idea, but it cannot be avowed because that would "complicate the moral issues of the cold war." Certainly the idea of rolling back

[11] Praeger, 1965, p. 138.
[12] *Ibid.,* p. 139.
[13] *Commonweal,* April 17, 1964.

Communism in Eastern Europe has long since been abandoned, and American policy for some time has been based on the hope of the liberalization from within with moral and economic encouragement from outside.

I believe we shall have to extend this same way of thinking to China and Cuba. Instead of trying to starve out Communism where it is established, we would do better to help a Communist nation to develop more quickly into the more stable and moderate stage of Communism. Who would be better off if either China or Cuba were thrown back into chaos and civil war with years of political anarchy and hopeless economic misery ahead and, in the case of Cuba, a return to a rightist tyranny? We might score a Cold War victory over Communism if such things happened but it would be a human defeat, for we would be in no position to control events, to establish a viable order that might be more free. We would take our chances, and China and Cuba would take their chances, with chaos, followed, in all probability, by new tyrannies; and these tyrannies would probably be less able than Communism to solve basic national problems, the solution of which is in the long run a precondition for a more free society.

There may well be need for much more of a focus, by the experts on Communist countries, on the ways in which the humanizing tendencies in those countries can be encouraged. I realize that neither time nor consumers' satisfactions automatically bring about these changes. Again, each country with its distinctive traditions and problems will have its own pilgrimage.

3. My third suggestion may have been implied in the second, but it has to do with our attitude toward the situation in which a nation still faces a choice between Communism and something else. Even in this situation, we should abandon the present axiom, on which American policy is based, that Communism is in all circumstances a worse choice than years of anarchy, of continuous civil war, or decades in which the basic social and economic problems of a nation go without serious attention, let alone any real solutions. Communism does produce governments that are effective in many ways. It does overcome anarchy. It does attend to the problems of hunger and poverty and disease and illiteracy. If it

were a permanent Stalinism, a government for an indefinite period based upon cruel terror and brainwashing, I should not be able to say what I have just said, but now I believe it must be said. The price paid for a limited time is great indeed, but seldom is the price of the alternatives weighed. The alternatives, being non-Communist, are assumed by definition to be better. But this is an ideological illusion.

If Americans can free themselves from this ideological illusion, it will be possible to see developments in Latin America with a sense of proportion. We would be able to avoid panic whenever revolutions in Latin America are led by various kinds of Marxists or when, as will always be the case, they win the support of disciplined Communists. It will be possible to distinguish between a national Communism, a Communism oriented toward the Soviet Union, and a Communism oriented toward Communist China. When such distinctions can be made, there is greater room for maneuver, and there may be a chance to encourage a national Communism that does not raise to the same extent the problem of American national security. Indeed, a Communism oriented toward Russia is in this respect less of a threat than a Communism oriented toward China. Actually, it may well be that freedom from frantic anti-Communism may enable the United States to help non-Communist revolutionary movements. At the present time, the absolutistic anti-Communism that controls American attitudes and policies in relation to Latin America makes us too inflexible to deal with the need for revolutionary change in those many neighboring countries.

4. Just as we should be discriminating about the revolutionary aspirations expressed in Marxist terms, we should be open to the new post-revolutionary generation of Marxists in Communist nations where they are beginning to gain some freedom of expression. By "we" I mean both Christians who have their arguments with Marxists and Americans who have their historic conflict with Communist countries.

One of the most fascinating vistas that are just opening up comes from the appearance of a new generation of Marxists who are asking questions, which their ideology had assumed to be closed. A correspondent, writing from Belgrade, reported, "In the last year, however, philosophers and writers of Yugoslavia, Hungary and Czechoslovakia have begun saying that Communism itself has created forms of alienation and will continue to create them." [14] This is, of course, a heresy so far as orthodox Communist doctrine is concerned. I have referred to Harvey Cox's comments about the interest in Christian theology among young Marxists in Czechoslovakia. The account of his discussion with Marxist intellectuals about this very matter of alienation is most interesting. He had read a paper, "Christian Responsibility in a Technological World," in Prague to a mixed group of Christians and Marxists, but he was astonished to find that he was more hopeful about the basically promising tendencies in technology than were the Marxists. They accused him of lacking "a feeling for the persistent alienation of man" which they said is "never solved politically." Here is the nub of all the Christian criticisms of Communist doctrine: it assumed that the Communist scheme, when politically established, would solve the human problems covered by such words as "alienation" which includes the conflict of man with man as well as the more ultimate forms of anxiety and guilt and lostness of man's existence. Cox writes: "When I cautiously suggested that they did not sound very 'Marxist' in their analysis, that if we were playing the script right, I should be the anguished Christian existentialist and they should be the clear-headed advocates of man's capacity to resolve his own problems, they roared and ordered another bottle of wine." [15] These indications of what is happening in Communist countries, in the relations of both Protestants and Catholics with Marxists, should be given great attention. The Cold War still impedes relaxed communication across the ideological boundaries, though among Communist countries Czechoslovakia, Hungary, Poland and Yugoslavia are not difficult to reach. The conversations between Christians and Communists in France and Italy are also important. Surely the time has come for putting great effort into both the official cultural exchanges and into the kind of informal

[14] David Hinde, *The New York Times,* Jan. 16, 1965.
[15] Harvey Cox, *The Correspondent,* Winter, 1965, p. 32.

dialogue about which Harvey Cox writes. This should be very high on the agenda of the churches.

5. This leads me to a final consideration concerning the relation between Christianity and Communism as faiths and ideas in conflict. Whatever the future of the international conflict, there will continue a spiritual conflict or at least a strongly competitive dialogue between Christians and Communists. As I have said before, it is a great mistake to identify this conflict with the conflict between nations. One obvious reason is that it must go on within nations quite as much as across national boundaries, but, more deeply, Christian responsibility in relation to Communists involves relationships and witness rather than the separation and hostility that international conflicts encourage.

God does not need defense against Communist atheism. A new generation of Communists for whom atheism is an inherited creed has begun to ask theological questions, and a new generation of Christians in East and West is also asking questions about its inherited conceptions and images of God. Official Communist atheism is a rigid position that is a response to false stereotypes of Christianity, and it has no word for anyone. A more serious problem is created by a self-sufficient scientism common to Communist and non-Communist nations alike.

The Christian Church has ahead of it a great new adventure, as it faces the post-revolutionary generation in Communist countries, as Communist fanaticism dies, and as these countries slowly become open to the outside world. American Christians can only have a part in these new opportunities for the church if they abandon their absolutistic anti-Communist crusade, if they take a positive attitude toward many of the social and economic results of the Communist revolution, and if they stand with open minds beside the people of those countries whose world is becoming more open. There are vistas here of listening and of witnessing and of new life for us all.

I have tried to be cautious in this chapter and have cited only those facts and tendencies which are widely attested. It should be made clear that they have no specifically Christian authentication. If what I have written is mistaken or so onesided as to be misleading, the reference to Christian perspective in my title gives it no authority. Faith and theology do not provide a factual picture of the world. If what I have written is essentially true, we may see some of its implications from the Christian perspective.

What I have said is a criticism of some uses of Christian faith as a weapon in the Cold War. It helps to deliver us from a false absolutism that denies or obscures the Christian perspective, the false absolutism of anti-Communism as the main consideration in many decisions. It helps to neutralize the temptation to self-righteousness, which is the most characteristic temptation of a nation. It counteracts the tendency to be willing to risk, out of ideological zeal, the existence of civilization, even the life of humanity, in nuclear war. It may enable us to discern the human on the other side of the present conflict and to establish relations with our neighbors in Communist countries. The question may be asked: what about Christian concern for the victims of Communism? That is a most important question. My answer is that those victims will be best helped as fanaticism is taken out of the Cold War, as Communist nations become humanized, and as the relations between them become looser. Victims will not be as much helped by efforts to liberate them by force as by the efforts to encourage liberalization within each Communist nation. And we must put beside the victims of Communism, the victims of anarchy and hunger in non-Communist countries and the possible victims in nuclear war. I believe in helping every nation to maintain its independence of Communist power and to find alternatives to Communist programs if this can be done in ways that are not self-defeating and are not likely to produce their own multitudes of victims.

I must not conclude a chapter on this subject at this time without at least suggesting a way of thinking about Communist China, which is the darkest cloud over the future, so far as the Cold War is concerned, in the minds of most people in the West. I do so with diffidence, because when there is so much uncertainty it is often better to remain silent.

Communism in China is certainly in its doctrinaire and fanatical stage, and Chinese national power, quite apart from Communism, must be seen as a threat to its neighbors. There is no policy we can project now that begins to seem adequate for the occasion.

We can hope that the same moderating tendencies that have appeared in European Communism will appear in Chinese Communism in due course. Also, internal success is more likely to favor such a development than internal frustration. Policies that are calculated to weaken or destroy the economy of China are likely to be self-defeating. It would be far better for the outside world to help China to move more quickly into the next stage of Communism in which she may become more moderate.

The American stance of moralistic hostility that seeks to keep China isolated from the international community is the worst possible approach to the problems which China raises. We should rather regard the Chinese revolution and all that has followed as a momentous human earthquake rather than as behavior to be judged by our usual moral yardsticks. It calls for awe initially rather than for condemnation. Here is the largest and one of the proudest of nations that has been the victim of exploitation and humiliation at the hands of the Western white world for generations and that has been too weak to defend itself, too disunited even to assert itself effectively. Now Communism has proved to be the instrument by which this nation has been united, by which it has achieved formidable national power, by which it has been catapulted into the modern world of technology. Also, China has been able under Communism to overcome the worst effects of its ancient poverty. Its women are full participants in the national life; its children are not put out to die, a sad and crude form of population control; its poor are no longer hopeless. Say what you will about the cost of the revolution, the cost of allowing the old social conditions to go unchanged needs to be weighed over against it. Communism needs to be seen as the instrument of modernization, of national unity, and of greater social welfare. The brainwashing, the cruel dealing with the opposition, and the political totalitarianism are the cost. At this stage, it is not for us to say whether we would or would not choose the effects at this cost. The changes have come. We should reject all the absolutistic doctrines and the utopian illusions that have accompanied them. But the real question is how the people of the West are to live with this great nation with its new unity and strength and hope.

I believe that Americans should seek to establish every type of relationship with China, diplomatic, economic, cultural, and human. Relations between churches is of course a main interest of Christians. China's ignorance of the outside world and American ignorance of what is happening in China are both destructive. There is no assurance that the inclusion of China in the United Nations would soon solve any problem, but it would at least be an advantage to have China present when she is a major factor in relation to so many issues that are discussed. Also this would help to overcome China's distorted views of other nations and of recent world history.

Nothing could illustrate more vividly the complete lack of empathy in official American attitudes toward China than the fact that the United States does near the borders of China what it would not tolerate near its own borders. This has been long-standing practice in the Formosa straits, but in the context of the war in Vietnam it has reached a new dimension. James Reston, who is always cautious as well as perceptive in his criticisms of American policy, writes as follows: "If the Chinese Communists had an expeditionary force of almost 200,000 men in southern Mexico and an air force capable of wiping out every city in the United States we would oppose it for a century, if necessary, but we have assumed that Hanoi and Peking would do otherwise." [16] Our government takes advantage of the present weakness of China to mount this force near her southern borders, while belligerent American citizens call for attacks on Chinese nuclear installations. When the Chinese respond to these threats with more than usually vituperative verbal attacks on the United States combined with more than usually wild elaborations of Chinese Communist doctrine, these are taken at face-value and used as one more argument for keeping China as isolated as possible. There is a vicious cycle here to which Communist China has made her own contribution, but the rigidity and lack of imagina-

[16] *The New York Times,* November 21, 1965.

tion of the government of the United States in dealing with China does much to perpetuate it. The excuse has often been made for American policy that the administration is imprisoned by public opinion, but recent studies of public opinion have shown that most Americans would follow the lead of the administration on this subject, and important elements in the business community are ahead of the government in their desire for commercial relations with Communist China.

No force that the United States can use in Asia can in the long run keep China from being the dominant power in her area, as the United States is in its area. It is better to gamble on policies that seek to neutralize the massive hostility of China against the West and especially against the United States than to gamble on the continuation of present attitudes and policies.

The United States should do what it can to strengthen China's neighbors that have the substance of nationhood and that have the will to be independent. This can be done without making any nation the instrument of an American ideological crusade against Chinese Communism. Certainly such nations as Japan and India and Pakistan and the Philippines, to name only a few, can be helped to preserve their independence. Vietnam, North and South, if we do not weaken them by bombing in a long war, can be a natural obstacle to Chinese expansion. I doubt if we can or should follow through on a policy of containment that emphasizes military power especially, that is relatively insensitive to the social and economic antidotes to the attraction of Chinese Communism, that fails to appreciate the significance of China's generations of frustrated pride as a nation and the depth of its resentment of such efforts by the white world to encircle it. In the meantime, there is some hope in the fact that China has consistently shown caution in its military moves. It has contented itself with the rounding out of its territory in terms of old Chinese claims on which the Nationalist government on Taiwan would agree with the government in Peiping. One of these claims is, of course, the claim to Taiwan as a part of China, and the United States does have responsibility to prevent the capture of that island and its integration with mainland China against the will of the inhabitants. This responsibility should not be confused with an anachronistic alliance with the Nationalist government which still makes the United States a party to the Chinese civil war. Already it is clear to most Americans that the United States does not regard Taiwan as a base for operations against the regime on the mainland, but I doubt if this is clear to the Chinese Communists.

We can hope for a new generation in China and the improvement of living conditions there to give China a stake in peace and stability, to moderate the fanaticism that goes with the early stage of Communism. The main questions with which we shall have to live are these: How can we encourage these favorable tendencies in China? How can we help China's neighbors to achieve and to maintain national strength with all possible natural and chiefly non-military checks on Chinese power? How can we, on our side, move away from the terrible hostility with which we approach China and do something to neutralize Chinese hostility to us? How can the isolation of China be overcome, which aggravates all the effects of Communist absolutism and frustrated national pride? How can an intractable division of the world between the white and the colored races be avoided? How can people in the United States become free to ask these questions about a nation of 700,000,000 persons instead of seeing China only as a Communist enemy to be contained by military power?

Postscript on the War in Vietnam. I have avoided any systematic discussion of the war in Vietnam in this book because the situation has changed so frequently and I have never stopped hoping that before it was published there would at least be an end to the fighting. As I write now this seems most unlikely. The United States has resumed the bombing of North Vietnam and the danger is very great that there will be considerable escalation of the war. I feel that in a book on this subject which contains so many references to contemporary events, I must state an attitude toward this war which is by far the chief source of anxiety in the sphere of foreign policy.

We need first to consider the present human costs of the war:

the suffering and death of an increasing number of Americans and of Vietnamese troops and also the cruel destructiveness of the war for the people of Vietnam, both North and South. The irony is that we probably bring greater suffering to the civilian population in South Vietnam than to the civilian population of North Vietnam. These human costs of the war may be said to be characteristic of all wars and the price we must pay to resist tyranny and aggression. In the case of the war against Hitler I argued so. But today I believe that the human cost of this war and the intrinsically evil actions to which it gives rise are leading us into a tragic blind alley.

Military successes are likely to lead to political and moral defeats. If the war lasts for years, as is now often predicted, it will destroy a large part of the country that we seek to save and it will so weaken the stamina of both North and South Vietnam that as one country or as two countries, Vietnam will not be a natural brake on the power of China. Also, after years of war we would be left the reluctant masters of a region that we do not understand; we would be cast in the role of imperialists even though our purposes are not imperialistic. We would be present with our military power near the borders of China as a threat in the eyes of the Chinese. All this would be after years in which everything that the United States has done or left undone has accentuated the resentments and the isolation of China. Events may carry us along into a major war on the continent of Asia and perhaps even into the Third World War and nuclear catastrophe. I do not expect the latter but it may come as the consequence of many limited steps.

The errors that have led us into this tragic blind alley have in large part been errors of presuppositions with which this chapter has dealt by implication. I shall mention three of these.

1. The first is the anti-Communist axiom that still controls American policy in Asia and Latin America though it has been abandoned by the government in relation to the Soviet Union and eastern Europe. This is the assumption that the worst fate that can come to any country is a Communist regime, worse than any rightist tyranny, worse than many years of civil war and

destructive disorder, worse than decades or generations of neglect of the country's social and economic problems. All that I have said about the fact that Communism is changing and pluralistic and capable of becoming after the early revolutionary period a constructive program bears on this. It raises the question as to what price the people of South Vietnam should pay to avoid a national Communism.

2. The second is the assumption that in Vietnam we have the test case for wars of liberation and that if we fail there we must expect such wars to succeed in many other places. The new emphasis on wars of liberation fails to distinguish sufficiently among different situations. For example, there may be a decisive difference between nations depending on the degree of viability of the society and the government, on the nation's capacity to develop a reasonably just alternative to Communism. In Vietnam we are in the position of creating a nation and this may be beyond our power. In other situations our responsibility may be to strengthen nations and governments which have a great deal of substance already. We hear much of the falling of dominoes; it is one thing to help prop up a domino but it is quite another to have to create a domino. To argue with desperation that if we fail to prevent the success of the "war of liberation" in Vietnam we will make it extremely difficult for nations to maintain their independence elsewhere is foolishly to undercut other efforts in far more promising situations.

Also we should reject the implication of so much of the discussion of wars of liberation that it is the American responsibility to engage in counter-revolutions against all wars of liberation on all continents!

I have had much to say in this chapter about the assumption that Communist power is primarily military power and how this always distorts the picture as we think of American policy in Asia. It causes American spokesmen to keep using the Munich analogy to defend our policy but this analogy is misleading because Hitler's power was primarily military power. The power of Communism is primarily the power to exploit weak social and political situations by using force but not by making a frontal military assault across borders. But the vulnerability of a country to this kind of exploitation makes all of the difference. There is maximum vulnerability at present in South Vietnam.

3. There has been a tendency to think of the American success in helping the nations of western Europe to defeat Hitlerism and to contain Stalinism as a model for Asian policy. One difference is the extent to which military power was primary in Europe, especially in the case of the defeat of Hitler. Another difference is that we were on the same wave length with the nations of western Europe whereas in Asia we fail to grasp the intangibles of Asian culture and there is the fact that there are self-defeating aspects of the military presence of a dominantly white nation on the continent of Asia. Also, in Europe we were supporting nations that had had stable governments and well organized economies; indeed, as I have said, they already had experienced two of the effects promised by the Communists: modernization and a high degree of social justice which made them invulnerable to the appeal of Communism. In Asia the main task is not military defense but the helping of nations to find another way to social revolution than the Communist way and this may not be possible for us to do unilaterally in South Vietnam. A vast enterprise of social engineering under military auspices may not take the place of an indigenous political movement as an alternative to Communism. These are factors which make the Munich analogy entirely misleading and they even make the defense of Europe by NATO no model for Asia.

Those who make policy and who are on the spot will have to find the next steps that may lead to an end of the fighting in Vietnam. However, it is doubtful if these steps will be taken unless official thinking changes concerning the presuppositions which underlie present policy. It is imperative that the United States continue to press for negotiations but this may well be futile unless we become more open to results of the negotiations that would be possible for the other side to accept. Calls for negotiations are often accompanied by policies which can well prevent them. So far the talk of unconditional negotiations has been accompanied by conditions concerning the parties with which we would negotiate and also by the clear implication that as a result of the negotiations there must be an independent South Vietnam in which the Vietcong which now controls most of the territory would have no role. The United States may be helped to discover an alternative to the present policy by allowing its actions to be multilaterally determined by the United Nations or by a conference which the United Nations may help to bring into being.

5: The Ethics of Force in the Nuclear Age

THE DISCOVERY of the power to annihilate whole nations would have created great dangers for humanity under any circumstances, but the dangers have been greatly aggravated by the fact that this discovery came when the world was divided by the absolute hostilities of the Cold War. The ordinary combination of egoisms and fears and resentments, and the habit of not doing enough in time to meet a problem, would have made it difficult in any case to live with this new power to destroy. In my last chapter, I said that as long as we saw on the other side of the conflict the threat of a centralized and permanent Stalinism we lived with the fear of permanent global slavery. And over against such permanent global slavery it did not seem totally irrational to risk global annihilation. There may have been something also in the words of the British nuclear scientist, P. M. S. Blacket: "Once a nation pledges its safety to an absolute weapon, it becomes emotionally essential to believe in an absolute enemy." [1]

In 1958, Professor Herbert Butterfield, speaking at American University in Washington, showed the error of this way of thinking. He said: "With modern weapons we could easily put back civilization a thousand years, while the course of a single century can produce a colossal transition from despotic regimes to a system of liberty." [2] Gradually there has been a change in the feeling about the absolute enemy and about the danger of global slavery. As I have said, the rhetoric of our most responsible leaders has changed. Absolute hostilities, at least in the context of European Communism, have eroded. The movement away from the Cold War at its worst was marked especially by an event connected

[1] Quoted in Christopher Driver, *The Disarmers, A Study in Protest,* Hodder and Stoughton, 1965, p. 95.
[2] Herbert Butterfield, *International Conflict in the Twentieth Century—A Christian View,* Harper, 1960, p. 95.

with nuclear power, the signing of the partial test ban treaty. This was only a hesitant first step toward control of the nuclear-arms race and nuclear disarmament, but it had immense symbolic importance, and it did end the collective madness of poisoning the atmosphere.

It is hardly necessary for me to say much about the new dimensions of violence and destruction that have come with nuclear weapons. There may be some debate as to whether or not it is possible technologically for a general war to annihilate mankind. There is little doubt about the possibility of destroying half of the population of nations that are immediate targets, and there is little doubt that fire and radioactivity would create a hell for most of the survivors. The side effects on other countries, especially in the northern hemisphere, would be colossal, and there are only dark guesses about the genetic damage to future generations. I have no intention of dwelling here on the familiar prospects of physical destruction.

I believe that inadequate attention has been given to the more intangible effects of nuclear war, the effects upon the morale of the survivors, on the possibilities of the recuperation of a nation and a culture, on the institutions of freedom which are often thought to be threatened more by Communism than by nuclear war. One reason that it has been difficult to attack this illusion about Communism as a greater threat to freedom than nuclear war is that it has been so widely believed that deterrence involving the risk of war would guard freedom against both threats, preventing both general war and the expansion of Communism. The events surrounding the Cuban missile crisis of 1962 and the consequences of the confrontation between the two great nuclear powers at that time give support to this idea. However, it should be said immediately that the success of that confrontation depended upon the extraordinary care and restraint shown on both sides when once the missiles were discovered by the American government. One cannot always expect such care and restraint.

Statistics about the dead give very little idea of the condition of the survivors of a nuclear holocaust or about the quality of a civilization that may emerge from it. I believe that Hans Morgenthau is more realistic on this matter than Herman Kahn, when he says, in criticism of Kahn's relative optimism about national recovery after a nuclear war, that only one who "is possessed not only by an extreme optimism but by an almost unthinking faith" can believe "civilization, any civilization, Western or otherwise, could survive such an unprecedented catastrophe." Morgenthau goes on to say: "The fundamental error in this reasoning to which I am referring, it seems to me, lies in the assumption that the moral fibre of a civilization has an unlimited capacity to recover from shock." [3] One can bracket with that statement of Morgenthau a similar statement by Reinhold Niebuhr that the "monstrous guilt" incurred in such a war might also morally destroy a civilization.[4] These are neglected dimensions of the results of nuclear war in all of the quantitative studies of the problem.

I have been surprised that Kahn who is personally very sensitive to all phases of the subject could allow himself in his writings to deal so abstractly with each particular type of quantitative effect of a major nuclear attack without examining the interaction between these effects. He even admits in the research underlying his book, *On Thermonuclear War*: "We did not look at the interaction of the effects we did study." And he goes on to say that his results depend on the assumption that reconstruction after a war is not "complicated by social disorganization, loss of personnel, radioactivity and so forth." And he admits that "if all these things happened together and all the other effects were added at the same time, one cannot help but have some doubts." [5]

Kahn's discussion of the genetic effects of a nuclear war has shocked me so much that I have wondered if he was not using his argument as chiefly an instrument of irony against nuclear war. He says it is an advantage that the genetic damage from a nuclear war will spread over tens of thousands of years. They would be too much for one generation to take. But what is to be said about the moral irresponsibility of acting in such a way as to injure the children of unborn generations on the basis of our own pre-

[3] *Commentary*, October 1961, p. 281.
[4] *Christianity and Crisis*, November 13, 1961.
[5] Princeton University Press, 1960, pp. 90-92.

carious political calculations? This is a *reductio ad absurdum* of all such calculations. And if each generation has its nuclear war, what would be the cumulative genetic effects? All of this makes nonsense of the assumption that Communism is a greater threat to humanity than nuclear war. Not only is Communism not inherited genetically but Communist children like other children already rebel against their parents' absolutism! That Kahn is not happy with his argument may be seen from his saying, "It is impossible to imagine a public figure stating, 'The damage due to fall out is not as serious as is sometimes implied, since most of the burden is borne by our descendents and not by our own generation.' While I believe that this statement is a defensible one, it is not one that I would care to defend in the give and take of public debate." [6]

Professor Morgenthau offers, as his ultimate rejection of nuclear war as a rationally chosen instrument of policy, his conclusion that such a war would destroy the meaning of life for the survivors who are secularists, who have no faith in God as transcending history.[7] There is truth in this view because of the extent to which the thoughtful secularists find meaning in life from hope for a better future for mankind. They might develop some form of private mysticism or religious cults that would be a source of healing and morale even in the face of such a catastrophe, as happened in the case of the mystery cults at the beginning of the Christian era. I doubt if there is a non-Biblical view of life that could give meaning to history under such circustances.

One issue that has been raised for Christian theology is whether or not Christian faith provides a guarantee that man cannot under any circumstances, even at a later stage of the technology of

[6] This discussion of the genetic effects of nuclear war is in *On Thermonuclear War*, pp. 43-54. Throughout the discussion, it is obvious that his one interest is in deterrence, which he regards as the best way to prevent the war. In his latest book, *On Escalation* (Praeger, 1965), his emphasis has shifted to the prevention of the higher levels of escalation. His relative optimism here is more convincing than his hopeful view of reconstruction after a full nuclear attack in the earlier book, though his faith in human rationality under stress is over-confident.

[7] "Death in the Nuclear Age," *Commentary*, September 1961.

weapons, destroy the race. Does the Christian necessarily believe that, after the worst man can do, God will still make something new in history, as on a smaller scale the Jews of the Old Testament in exile expected God to redeem at least a remnant after the destruction of their national life? I doubt if we can assume as a Christian dogma that at some stage in the development of weapons and at a corresponding stage in the development of human folly and sin it may be impossible for man to destroy all that makes the human race human, perhaps to end the chance for this planet to sustain our kind of life. I am not suggesting that this is probable or that it is even possible now. Christian faith has always seen man as a pilgrim on this earth without worldly security. The New Testament Christians looked for a new heaven and a new earth that would come by a saving act of God. Modern men have assimilated the idea that cosmic forces at some point in the distant future would probably end the earth's capacity to support human life. But neither of these prospects is the same as the prospect of man's having the freedom to destroy himself and to end God's experiment with man on this planet.

After the dropping of the atomic bombs on Japan, a Commission appointed by what was then the Federal Council of Churches (which was later absorbed into the National Council of Churches), under the chairmanship of Professor Robert L. Calhoun, was asked to prepare a report on the theological and ethical implications of atomic war. The Commission considered this whole problem of the relation between God's providence and man's freedom in history. The majority of the Commission, which was made up of many of the best known Protestant theologians of the period, found that they could not say it was impossible for man in his folly and sin to destroy himself. This was believed to be one of the consequences of the freedom God had given to us.

The issue is well put in the following passage of this report, which was drafted by Professor Calhoun: "Suppose then that in a sudden tempest of atomic warfare human civilization or even all earthly human life were extinguished, by the acts of some men. The fatal decisions would be human decisions, not divine fiats. In so far as divine justice contributed to the outcome, it would be through the active preservation of dependable order. Nothing else than this could be regarded as consistent with the dependability of God. But the persons thus suddenly ending their lives on earth would come to the end in different roles, some as active aggressors, and others as relatively innocent victims. This contrast is always present in massive man-made disasters, and poses in itself no new problem. But the inclusiveness and finality of a possible global annihilation puts the old problem with fresh urgency. How, in the face of such a cataclysm, is the mercy of God—nay, even the justice of God, in any personal sense—to be seen?"

The answer finally came to this: "His [God's] creating and redeeming work will not end even if the earth be destroyed, and whatever men have done, whatever of human existence has been good, He will cherish forever. . . . Finally, it is a part of our Christian faith that not only the high moments of men's lives but their very existence and fellowship as personal selves is safe in God's hands; that death is swallowed up in the victory we call the resurrection so that death is not the last word." [8]

Whatever the excuse for contributing to the risks of nuclear war, must we not say that for men to act in such a way as to bring nearer the doom of mankind in history is to be guilty of final disobedience to the God of life and love, and of ultimate treason to humanity? I believe that the answer can only be "yes." And I realize I share the corporate disobedience and treason when I go on to say that there are complications in immediately renouncing the possession of nuclear weapons. I shall discuss those complications and then suggest an *interim* strategy.

The first and most natural response to this situation is the advocacy of total renunciation of nuclear weapons "without tarrying for any." This would involve both personal conscientious objection against any part in the production or preparation for use, as well as the use, of such weapons, and it would involve the public demand for total nuclear disarmament, multilateral disarmament preferably, unilateral disarmament if that fails. This

[8] This report appeared as a supplement to *Social Action*, April 1946, published by what was then the Council for Social Action of the Congregational Christian Churches.

response of nuclear pacifism is quite common in many countries, especially in Japan, Germany, Britain, and Holland. It is often inspired by Christian convictions, but Christian nuclear pacifists are usually part of a larger movement that has many spiritual inspirations. There is less nuclear pacifism in the United States than in most countries in which public opinion has great freedom. I suspect the reason is that the United States has the only nuclear power available to offset the nuclear power of the Soviet Union, and that nuclear pacifism in this country must imply immediately and unambiguously a political act of renunciation of that power. Nuclear pacifists in other countries may believe that the United States should take such action, but some are fuzzy about this and are clearer in their conviction that they do not want their own countries to have nuclear weapons. Among other things, they do not want their nations to become natural targets for nuclear weapons. They are remote from having to face the actual alternatives that American citizens and the American government must face. Until one's own decision makes the difference of having or not having any power to balance the decisive power of the Soviet Union, it is hard to realize fully what the issues are. Quite apart from any ideological considerations, I think a complete monopoly of the decisive form of military power in the hands of any nation or alliance of nations would cause grave concern to many people strongly attracted by nuclear pacifism. There are, of course, many nuclear pacifists and also absolute pacifists in non-Communist countries who would reject in principle any reliance on the American nuclear deterrent. I have no intention of making light of that fact, but I have noticed that this fully consistent nuclear pacifism in practice shades into the fuzzier position that I have described.

The strength of this broad tendency toward nuclear pacifism can be seen in the fact that the Vatican Council has been a sounding board for it in spite of the Roman Catholic fear of Communism. The statement about nuclear war in Schema XIII which created a great stir partly reflects this tendency though it avoids the moral demand for immediate unilateral abandonment of nuclear weapons. It describes the devastation that would be produced by nuclear war. It gives no sanction to military policies based on the idea of nuclear deterrence and warns against the confidence that deterrence will safeguard peace. It is strongest in its prohibition of military strategies that are directed toward the destruction of populations as in the following passage:

All these considerations compel us to undertake an evaluation of war with an entirely new attitude. The men of our time must realize that they will have to give a somber reckoning for their deeds of war. For the course of the future will depend largely on the decisions they make today.

With these truths in mind, this most holy Synod makes its own the condemnations of total war already pronounced by recent Popes, and issues the following declaration:

Any act of war aimed indiscriminately at the destruction of entire cities or of extensive areas along with their population is a crime against God and man himself. It merits unequivocal and unhesitating condemnation.

The unique hazard of modern warfare consists in this: it provides those who possess modern scientific weapons with a kind of occasion for perpetrating just such abominations. Moreover, through a certain inexorable chain of events, it can urge men on to the most atrocious decisions. That such in fact may never happen in the future, the bishops of the whole world, in unity assembled, beg all men, especially government officials and military leaders, to give unremitting thought to the awesome responsibility which is theirs before God and the entire human race.[9]

---

[9] To get the full force of the Council's statement it is important to refer to its remarkable call for laws which provide for the conscientious objector to modern war: "Moreover, it seems right that laws make humane provisions for the case of those who for reasons of conscience refuse to bear arms, provided however, that they accept some other form of service to the human community." It should be remembered that because Catholic teaching has never supported absolute pacifism, this provision for the conscientious objector must apply to those who, while not absolute pacifists, object to particular wars, perhaps especially nuclear wars. These words can now be invoked by the American Catholics who oppose the war in Vietnam as an immoral war. They suggest that the United States should move toward some

I confess that I often envy those who can accept nuclear pacifism and who believe without any qualifications in immediate nuclear disarmament, unilateral if necessary, and who refuse to allow themselves to be caught in the dilemma of deterrence. I do not suppose life is any simpler for them, especially in the United States, but it is easier for them to have a view of what the nation should do that is intellectually and morally consistent.

I have already said something about the difficulties I find in pacifism as a political position, and I think that nuclear pacifism when the decisive forms of military power are nuclear shares in these difficulties. I am unwilling to give up the general position that no type of power should be allowed to go unchecked, if it is possible to prevent it. The balance of nuclear power has helped to preserve a precarious peace for some years. It has had the effect of setting limits to the expansion of the Soviet Union and has been one factor in turning that country to its present emphasis on peaceful co-existence and competition. For the United States to give up nuclear weapons unilaterally would tempt the Soviet Union to move into a vast vacuum, not by direct nuclear attacks or by invasion but by many more limited forms of pressure against the background of the nuclear threat. If we were able to get an objective view of the world, I think Americans would see that, though they have no aggressive intentions, it is fortunate that the United States has no monopoly of nuclear power.

If this country were to disarm unilaterally, would it not in a crisis be driven to desperate self-defense, to efforts to reactivate some of its nuclear capability? Is it not likely that this effort would at least bring upon the nation that engaged in it nuclear punishment or at least the threat of nuclear punishment from the nations that had not disarmed? I ask this because I wonder if unilateral nuclear disarmament would even prevent nuclear war at least on a reduced scale which might bring a terrible punishment for the nation weakened by disarmament. Also, there is a

---

legal provision for those who conscientiously oppose particular wars as well as for absolute pacifists, difficult as this may be administratively. Pressure from Roman Catholics in this country for such a provision will be quite a new factor.

better chance to achieve a multilateral solution of the problem of nuclear armaments if no nation has a monopoly, and so I doubt if it is in the interests of general nuclear disarmament to disarm unilaterally. Unilateral steps toward disarmament in the hope that the other side will reciprocate are important. President Kennedy's announcement in June 1963 that the United States would discontinue nuclear tests, unless the Russians tested, was an example of this kind of action, and it led to the partial test ban treaty a short time later. A great variety of initiatives, entered into with ingenuity and with provisional faith and with risk (and there are risks in not taking such steps), are essential. However, within limits it is still possible to say that the presence of the power to deter does help to prevent the war in which nuclear weapons might be used. Certainly we cannot trust to this alone, and the line may be a thin one that separates deterrence from provocation. The prevention of a monopoly of decisive power on either side does help to preserve a wide area in which many nations have considerable freedom of movement.

There is another phase of the matter which keeps nuclear pacifism from being a self-sufficient policy. I have already referred to this in my discussion of the limits of pacifism in general. There is no possibility psychologically or politically for the United States to choose unilateral nuclear disarmament. Those who personally believe that abstractly this would be the better choice should admit that it is the responsibility of the American government to guard the nation against nuclear blackmail or nuclear attack unless there is a radical change in the convictions held by the vast majority of citizens. Quite apart from the conflicts of the Cold War, this would still be a government's responsibility so long as there is no genuinely effective structure of collective security and so long as there is another nation, not fully trusted, that has nuclear armaments. If there comes to be less mutual distrust between the nuclear powers than there is, I hope that it will be possible to run much greater risks in seeking a way out of the dilemma.

In view of this situation it would seem to me that the nuclear pacifist would have to regard his position as limited in political applicability, that he must recognize the need of an interim strategy that takes account of the responsibilities of government in the situation as it is. He may seek to bring about a revolution in public opinion that would change the alternatives open to the government, and this is in principle possible, but there is no indication that such a change will take place either in relation to American national defense or in relation to the clearest American commitments to defend other nations. We must live and decide and act as a nation now. I need not say again that all of this needs to be understood in the light of a realistic understanding of the reasonable fears of other nations.

My conclusion so far is that there is no way of escaping from the moral burden of possessing nuclear weapons, of seeking to preserve a precarious balance of nuclear power in the world. We need to do this both to discourage the pressures or the initial aggressions that might trigger general war and to prevent other nations from taking the short cut of military threat or aggression to extend their power over their neighbors. Much depends on the priority that we give to these two purposes. So far as the possession of nuclear armaments is concerned I think that the first should have priority, both because a general war is the greatest of all threats to humanity, even to freedom (if the argument in my last chapter is at all sound) and because nuclear weapons are only remotely relevant to the likely forms of Communist penetration or expansion. Indirect aggression or the taking advantage by Communists of revolutionary situations in politically and socially vulnerable nations can only be met by limited uses of force combined with ideas and a constructive revolutionary program as an alternative to Communism. I realize there is a more shadowy factor here that comes from the kind of fear that the possession of a few bombs by Communist China might have in discouraging any kind of political resistance to Chinese pressure. Merely to know that China has no nuclear monopoly would be reassuring at this point.

After we have said all of these things about the possession of a nuclear armament versus unilateral nuclear disarmament, we are left with an appalling dilemma. We may have to say "yes" to the possession of these weapons but, if they are ever used in a general nuclear war, they will destroy all that their possession is intended to defend. Sometimes the depth of this dilemma is hidden by the assumption that if we are resolute enough to make our deterrent credible, the other side will always yield. Much of the willingness to defend the use of nuclear weapons is based upon the assumption that if the people on our side show enough toughness, enough readiness to use them, they will never have to be used. This has been true so far, and we have to thank the nuclear realism of the Russians plus the basic tactical patience of Communists who have had enough confidence in their reading of history to enable them to retreat for the moment in order to advance at a more favorable time. But how can we count on this favorable result if the leaders on the other side happen to be less realistic or less cool-headed than has been the case, or if they feel their national security gravely threatened? Moreover, American leaders might become too heady if they came to believe that they could get away with more and more pressure on other nations. This would increase the risk of war, and it would also be a temptation to our side to abuse its power. There is a momentum in the exercise of military power when those branches of government that concentrate on it gain independence of public opinion in a crisis. The belief in national righteousness may easily obscure the temptation to take unjust advantage of such a situation.

The depth of the dilemma is also partly hidden by a strangely optimistic view of the rationality of nations under stress, the rationality of both sides in a conflict. The fact that rational restraint has been observed by both sides in many situations, for example in Korea and in Vietnam where there have been no direct attacks on the territory of either of the major nuclear powers, may be misleading. I need only mention the nightmare ahead, if the proliferation of nuclear weapons enables many nations to create nuclear incidents that might start a general holocaust.[10]

[10] Readers should not miss the table of forty-four rungs on the ladder of escalation in Herman Kahn's *On Escalation, op. cit.,* p. 39. Though ultimately Kahn may have too much confidence in the rationality of governments under

I shall now deal with some possible moral landmarks in this deeply perplexing situation. We can expect military conflicts. We should fear all-out war as possible even though not only unthinkable but beyond our imagination. We can have no idea of what it would be like to survive it. The most natural prudential limiting of violence is needed within the structure of deterrence, which cannot be wished out of existence, but also there need to be strong moral pressures against the perpetration of unlimited violence against other peoples. I have missed any serious discussion of these moral pressures in the United States apart from the discussion that comes to expected conclusions in pacifist circles. Roman Catholic moral theologians have done something to raise the moral issues, because they have made the idea of the "just war," which includes the idea of the limited war, an explicit part of their teaching. The "just war" as a guiding principle belongs to Christian ethics generally and also to the public ethics of Christendom, though, so far as deciding that particular wars waged by one's own nation are unjust, it is more honored in the breach than in the observance. My own limited contacts with people who are close to the making of military policy leads me to believe that as individuals they are often very sensitive about the moral implications of nuclear war. Professor Paul Ramsey has done more than any other Protestant theologian to raise the moral question about the use of nuclear weapons or any other weapons of mass destruction.

We can hardly exaggerate the effects of what I have elsewhere called the "corporate fall" [11] that took place during the second half of the Second World War, when it came to be taken for granted that direct attacks, which saturated great cities and their

stress, so long as there are only a few nuclear powers with much at stake and great experience in prudent self-limitation, there is some ground for the hope that the higher levels of escalation may be avoided, even if the nuclear stage of a war begins.

[11] I have used this phrase in describing the use of weapons of mass destruction in the Second World War in my *When Christians Make Political Decisions*, Association Press, 1964, p. 79. I have also discussed this whole issue in my chapter in the volume edited by me, *Nuclear Weapons and the Conflict of Conscience*, Scribners, 1962.

populations with explosions and fire, were permissible. The Western Allies, especially Great Britain and the United States, bombed such cities as Hamburg, Dresden, Berlin, Tokyo in this way before the United States took responsibility for using the first atom bombs on Hiroshima and Nagasaki. A volume appeared in England in 1963 entitled *The Destruction of Dresden,* which is a sign of the present moral revulsion against the British policy of obliteration bombing in the Second World War. The favorable reception of the book in Britain reflects this attitude. It is published with a Foreword by Air Marshal Sir Robert Saundby who was second in command at the time of the bombing of Dresden, and the author, David Irving, had the cooperation of the former Commander-in-chief of the Royal Bomber Command that was immediately responsible for the raids on Dresden. A memorandum by Winston Churchill is quoted as expressing doubts about these and similar raids, even though as Prime Minister he had supported them. Churchill's reasoning is of great interest: "It seems to me that the moment has come when the question of bombing of German cities simply for the sake of increasing the terror, *though under other pretexts,* should be reviewed. Otherwise we shall come into control of an utterly ruined land." [12] This is not the full moral argument connected with the idea of the "just war," but behind that concept there is great emphasis historically on responsibility for the peace that follows the war, and in a rough way Churchill reflected that. Indeed it was wholly characteristic of him to do this. There is a curious contrast between British initiative in obliteration bombing and American initiative in calling for unconditional surrender. Both were reckless policies in relation to the peace.

I have often reflected on the fact that two Americans of great integrity and of the most humane spirit were chiefly responsible

[12] *The Destruction of Dresden,* William Kimber, London, 1963, p. 229. (Italics mine.) A similar concern was recently expressed by General Maxwell Taylor in connection with the idea of bombing Hanoi. He said, "I wouldn't think we would want to bomb Hanoi. I think that we need the leadership in Hanoi to be intact to make those essential decisions we hope they will make sometime." (*The New York Times,* November 23, 1965.)

for the decision to drop the atomic bombs on Japan. I refer to President Truman and Secretary Stimson. They did it conscientiously because they believed that that decision would shorten the war, make unnecessary the invasion of Japan, and save hundreds of thousands of lives on both sides. While I can only respect their consciences, I think this action was part of a general tendency to assume that any degree of violence against any targets, without regard to who the victims may be, is permissible, if those who are responsible calculate that it will make military victory more likely. No one said that the idea of moral limits in warfare was to be abandoned; it was abandoned and the world learned that this was the way in which nations can be expected to act under pressure.

Today, it is taken for granted that massive attacks on populations are not to be preferred; indeed, there has been a strong tendency to emphasize limited war, counter-force war, graduated deterrence in the hope that cities may be spared. Yet, if the worst comes to the worst the annihilation of the adversary's centers of population remains a live option at a late stage in the escalation of a war. I realize that what Secretary MacNamara says, after he supports limited and counter-force war, about what our nation is poised to do in destroying the enemy's populations and the substance of its corporate life is now chiefly tough talk and part of a war of nerves, and I have no doubt he and others who speak as he does believe that such tough talk accompanying full power to destroy as a deterrent will prevent nuclear war. Perhaps it will, in this moment of history, but what are the moral implications of threats that indicate that under some circumstances behavior of the kind threatened is morally permissible? What will be the effects of this upon the moral sensitivities of a nation?

These issues, as I write, are not matters of speculation that belong to an indefinite future. They are serious issues in connection with the conduct of the war in Vietnam. To be sure, there is no expectation that nuclear weapons will be used and this fact may remind us that the moral issue of total war is not related to nuclear weapons alone. The nation is told there is no intention of bombing Hanoi and other population centers in North Vietnam, though many villages are bombed in South Vietnam because they are suspected of harboring the Vietcong. The administration has maintained a policy of restraint, especially in relation to North Vietnam. And yet there cannot but be an uneasy feeling that, under some future conditions, the decision might be made to bomb the northern cities. If this takes place it will prove that the United States has learned nothing from the moral failure in the Second World War. A column in *The Evening Star* in Washington, D.C., by Charles Bartlett twice used the word "pulverization" to describe what critics of the administration were asking it to do in North Vietnam (July 13, 1965). I was astonished at a statement by Lieutenant General Samuel T. Williams, who commanded American forces in Vietnam from 1955-1960, in which he advocated the "bombing of dikes and dams on the Red River, north and west of Hanoi." He said this would put Hanoi under a couple of feet of water, as well as much of the industrial complex along the Red River Valley. He added that "this would hurt them badly." [13] I am sure the General is horrified by atrocities he attributes to the Communists, but this would be an unspeakable atrocity. Fortunately General Williams, now retired, has nothing to do with the decisions of the United States government, and such a wicked action is almost certainly far from the intentions of President Johnson. The horrifying thing is that such an idea should be bandied about in military circles. There are many people in the United States (doubtless a large proportion of them conventional churchmen, for the church has made little direct effort to provide an antidote to this kind of thinking) who stand ready to advocate the greatest crimes, if they are perpetrated in the name of freedom.

Those responsible for strategy are caught in a trap that is most fateful for us all. They do prefer to keep military operations limited in any war, limited to conventional weapons, limited as to the targets at which they aim; but, at the same time there is a doctrine, sound as far as it goes, that both sides should have their bases and their retaliatory forces as invulnerable as possible. The ground for this is that in a rational world no one will

[13] Interview published in *Oakland Tribune,* Aug. 20, 1965.

start a nuclear war or the nuclear stage of a war unless he can strike effectively at the enemy's bases; therefore, such a war is not likely to be started, and the world is likely to have a measure of stability.

The other side of the picture is gradual escalation; with other and perhaps less responsible nuclear powers capable of triggering the nuclear stage of the war, and with the panic and the lack of communication between adversaries, these rational limits may not be observed. There is a danger that in desperation one side will strike the other's cities, which can be reached, if the bases are invulnerable.

In other words, this situation of stability growing out of the approximate invulnerability of the retaliatory striking force of both sides may be the best way of preventing nuclear war under present conditions, but, if this arrangement should fail, the door is opened to the bombing of populations. Remember that, once a war has started, the checks from outside on a small group of policy-makers within the government become minimal. This is illustrated by the fact that the American people did not even know there were atomic bombs before they learned about the bombing of Hiroshima and Nagasaki after the event.

I have tried to state the dreadful nature of our present dilemma. Unilateral abandonment of the means of nuclear deterrence is politically impossible, and it cannot be defended as the surest way to prevent war as of now. As I have said, quite apart from the Cold War and the threat of Communist expansion, it would probably be wrong to allow any nation to have a monopoly of nuclear power. Yet if the deterrence system should fail, though there may be a period of prudent restraints, neither side has been prepared by strong moral restraints against the annihilation of the other's population. I do not mean that individuals do not have such moral restraints, but these are likely to be overruled by the momentum of events and by progressive self-deception. An article in *The New York Times,* on July 7, 1965, revealed the inner moral protests of an American pilot in Vietnam together with the process by which they were silenced. "I do not like to hit a village," said one of the pilots who has flown more than 100 missions. "You know you are hitting women and children, too. But you've got to decide that your cause is noble and that the work has to be done." This illustrates the process perfectly, though the scale of the operation was small. Also conventional weapons were used, and the operation was defended on the ground that the killing of non-combatants was only a side effect from the intended killing of Vietcong. But the same mental process can be expected, when a decision is made to destroy a city as the main target.

This whole subject is one on which it becomes more difficult each day to speak, because words and more words seem so weak in relation to the moral horrors and absurdities about which they are used. Recognizing the difficulty of speaking without obscuring the very things about which I speak, I shall emphasize what I call two moral landmarks that may guide thought and decision in the use of weapons and the choice of targets.

The first is the moral necessity of rejecting in advance all warfare that is directed primarily against populations or against the national substance of another nation. Professor Paul Ramsey bears down hard on the one point that, at all costs, the essential "moral immunity" of non-combatants must be preserved. In this he follows traditional Christian teaching about the "just war." He seeks to avoid the tendency that he finds in most moralists, Catholic and Protestant, to emphasize only the principle of proportionality in the use of violence. This broad principle means merely that we should not engage in acts of destruction that are out of proportion, in the evil done, to the good in the ends that can be achieved. This seems to him to be too slippery a concept without sufficient sure guidance; whereas, to emphasize the moral immunity of non-combatants is to present an absolute guideline for policy that cannot be obscured. He scouts the notion that today there is no distinction between combatants and non-combatants. In practice, his view means that in any city there are enough people who are not combatants, children and old people especially and also many others whose lives are only marginally related to the waging of war, to make it morally necessary to spare the city as the object of direct attack. Indeed, there may well be more of these non-combatants in a nuclear war, which is likely to be short, involving the use of weapons already in existence, than in a long war, in which so much of the civilian population is engaged in the manufacture of weapons and other materials of war.

Many of these people, apart from the children, may not be subjectively innocent. They may hate and they may will the destruction of the enemy's population by the combatants who represent them. Indeed, they may be less innocent subjectively than the young men who are drafted into the armed forces. This is one aspect of the matter that troubles me most, and I fear that the principle of non-combatant immunity, when isolated as the most significant moral principle of restraints, may cause people to be too uncritical of methods of war so long as they lead only to the annihilation of the relatively innocent young men who happen to fill the combatant role. This has bearing on the use of tactical nuclear weapons on the battlefield, which, among other things, may destroy or distort the reproductive capacity of all who are within range.

However, Ramsey's use of the traditional distinction between combatants and non-combatants is one way of establishing the position that direct attack on cities is out of bounds. There are enough non-combatants in them to serve as benign hostages. Ramsey's position turns out in his most recent writings to be less helpful as a clear guide to strategists because of the great stress he now puts on "collateral damage." This is only a way of stating the familiar principle of "doubt effect." According to this principle, it is immoral to launch an attack directly and intentionally against populations, but it is morally permissible to attack a military target, even though many civilians live in the same area and will be killed. When this principle is applied to nuclear war, the fire-storms and fall-out and many of the after-effects of bombing will lead to the destruction of civilians on a large scale and bring great misery to survivors. The principle of "collateral damage" under these circumstances renders more imprecise than ever the principle of the moral immunity of non-combatants. Actually those who think in these terms, including Ramsey, must fall back upon the principle of proportionality and consider how much damage done to civilians can be justified in order to seek out the bases and the centers of military force and destroy them. The danger is that the criteria will become too subjective and that almost any destruction will be permitted if it is not intended.

Use of the principle of non-combatant immunity can be a guide in the early stages of escalation in a war. Although it is less emphasized than prudential political considerations, I am sure that it is an important factor in preventing the United States from bombing Hanoi. Yet, the more advanced the escalation, the greater the difficulty in making this distinction in practice, when populations are the victims of collateral damage.

This principle of collateral damage helps Ramsey to justify a policy of deterrence based upon the possession of any weapons, which can be used either for the bombing of military targets *or* for the bombing of cities. The manufacture of them for the former use can be justified; and, even when they are used only for that limited purpose, the enemy can expect to be exposed to unacceptable damage to cities, even when our side may not intend such damage. Otherwise, Ramsey would find it gravely immoral even to threaten to do what is immoral. The threat is implicit in the well known fact of collateral damage, and Ramsey in his most recent writings seems to take some satisfaction that he can have an armament for deterrence on a moral basis. Since I cannot renounce the possession of deterrent power, as of now, I cannot reject this argument altogether, but I fail to take the moral satisfaction in it that I find in Ramsey's most recent discussion. He uses such a phrase as "just targeting" with too great ease, knowing that the collateral damage from "just targeting" may be widespread destruction of populations. He too readily makes such "just targeting" a rationalization of a military policy that none of the issues at stake between nations can justify. The fact that he does not renounce the stereotypes of thinking connected with the Cold War may affect his sense of how much damage can be justified as a product of "just targeting." Yet, he draws back from what at first seems to be the drift of his thought and he says that the higher levels of "lethal fall-out" as collateral damage go beyond a proportionate use of force "and beyond the rational ordering of force to a political purpose." [14]

Ramsey has revealed the nature of the problem more clearly and starkly than anyone else, but his doing so has in fact forced him back to great reliance on the principle of proportionality so far as the actual conditions of large scale nuclear war are concerned. I think that he should put more emphasis than he does on such considerations as the fabric of community and the recuperative capacity of a nation. If these are destroyed as a result of collateral damage, the whole distinction between just targeting and collateral damage is reduced to an absurdity. To stress the permissibility of just targeting, as much as Ramsey does, with indeterminate collateral damage may undercut the moral inhibition against escalation.

Against this background, the Christian churches should say to the state that any strategies that have as their effect the destruction of populations on a large scale and that render another nation unable to recover are murderous, out of all bounds theologically and morally, incapable of justification by any political calculation. Secretary MacNamara, who has done so much to shift the emphasis from preparation for all-out nuclear war to preparation for counter-forces war and especially for limited conventional war, seemed to fall into this kind of threatening when he spoke of our capability to "destroy the aggressor as a viable society" even after a well-planned and executed surprise-attack on our forces.[15] As I have said before, this kind of talk is part of a war of nerves, and Mr. MacNamara doubtless believes that to engage in it from time to time will prevent any such events from taking place. But such words cannot be separated from a habit of thinking, which they encourage in the nation.

Even if one's view of Christian ethics seeks to avoid particular moral absolutes from which can be deduced specific policies, regardless of the circumstances, there are some moral limits beyond which we should not go, regardless of any calculations. In the context of foreign policy, much is made of an ethic of respon-

[14] *Peace, the Churches and the Bomb,* pp. 50-54.
[15] *The New York Times,* Feb. 16, 1965.

sibility in contrast to an ethic that stresses personal purity, personal non-participation in evil. Often this is influenced by Max Weber's contrast between an ethic of ultimate ends and an ethic of responsibility. He illustrates the first by referring to the "Christian who does rightly and leaves the results to the Lord" and the second by one who "has to give an account of the foreseeable results of one's action." I agree with the importance of this contrast, and this book has been written on the basis of what is hoped to be an ethic of responsibility. However, there are degrees of moral evil; and, some individual deeds may be so clearly wrong that no one should allow calculation that gives some rationalization for them to become a basis for permitting them. We come up against a moral boundary, and I believe that this is the case with war against populations. Max Weber himself recognizes that such boundaries exist; when a man acts by following an ethic of responsibility he may "somewhere reach the point where he says: 'Here I stand; I can do no other.' " He says that "every one of us who is not spiritually dead must realize the possibility of finding himself at some point in that position." And he adds: "Insofar as this is true, an ethic of ultimate ends and an ethic of responsibility are not absolute contrasts but rather supplements, which only in unison constitute a genuine man—a man who *can* have the 'calling for politics.' " [16]

Certainly a Christian ethic that has no place for this cannot be recognizable as such. Also a Christian who understands the degrees of self-deception of which he is capable will stop before he allows the calculations that are the mark of responsibility to allow him to sanction or support the destruction of populations. In addition to the tendency toward self-deception, there is the consideration that, when finite men calculate concerning the complicated consequences of their acts, the certainty that one possible decision is overwhelmingly evil may cause us to be skeptical about

[16] This discussion by Max Weber is in an essay entitled "Politics as a Vocation" included in the volume *From Max Weber: Essays in Sociology,* translated and edited by H. H. Gerth and C. Wright Mills, Oxford University Press, 1946. There is a pamphlet edition of the same English translation, edited by Franklin Sherman and published by the Fortress Press in 1965.

the calculations that would cause us to sanction this evil for the sake of the more uncertain prevention of a greater evil, the scope of which is not clearly known. Under such conditions, it may indeed be responsible to say "no" and leave "the results to the Lord." Governments may not know the Lord, but they may sense the dimensions of the evil. Churches that evade the issue are guilty of a grave default.

A second landmark in our discussion of the ethics of force in the nuclear age should be the resolute refusal to be the first to use nuclear weapons. This applies to tactical nuclear weapons as well as megaton bombs in strategic warfare. I realize we cannot say that, under all circumstances in the future, nuclear weapons of all kinds, which may be limited and precise and with minimal fall-out, are inherently worse than all conventional weapons, however destructive they may be. My references to the bombing of Hanoi with conventional weapons and to the bombing of the cities of Germany and Japan before atomic weapons became available underline this point. Yet one of the important facts about nuclear weapons is that there is a recognized threshold connected with their use that under present conditions seems to be the chief break on the ultimate escalation of a conflict. Professor Henry Kissinger, who was one of the first to advocate the inclusion of tactical nuclear weapons in American armament in Europe, has come to see the danger here. He says: "The dividing line between conventional weapons is more familiar and therefore easier to maintain—assuming the will to do so—than any distinction within the spectrum of nuclear weapons.[17] Herman Kahn in his table of the ladder of escalation groups the forty-four rungs under six basic thresholds. He says that "of the six basic thresholds, the nuclear seems the most salient, the most widely acknowledged, and quite possibly the most likely to be observed." He quotes Alain Enthoven, Deputy Assistant Secretary of Defense, as follows: "In efforts to limit violence, there is and will remain an important distinction, a 'fire-break' if you like. . . . a recognizable, qualitative distinction that both combatants can

[17] *The Necessity of Choice,* Harper & Row, 1960, pp. 82-83.

recognize and agree upon if they want to." This is the nuclear threshold.[18]

The United States at this time in its history should at least determine not to be the first to initiate the nuclear stage of a conflict. China is on record to this effect; if there is a tendency to discount this in the West, it could be recognized as consistent with the military caution that has always characterized Chinese policy and strategy.[19] There is a case for the possession of nuclear weapons to deter their use by another nation. But there is no political or moral objective that can justify any nation in initiating the nuclear stage of a war. How weapons should be used by a nation that is attacked is another problem. We can be sure they should not be used against centers of population or to "destroy the aggressor nation as a viable society." I have little confidence that they would not be so used under the most extreme pressure of events, but principles of restraint might result in the postponement of their use in this way except as a last resort; this gaining of time might actually prevent the ultimate catastrophe. The deterrent effect of having nuclear weapons may come chiefly from the fact that no potential adversary can be sure how the weapons will be used against it, if it should first use nuclear weapons. Nuclear weapons should exist only to deter the use of nuclear weapons.

Anything would be better than for one's nation to be the one that initiates the nuclear stage of a war, making itself a nation of destroyers on so vast a scale and running the risk of ending most of the continuities of corporate life in at least the northern hemisphere, running this risk for other peoples who have no part in the decision and for unborn generations.

The chances of avoiding counter-city warfare, if nuclear war ever gets far advanced, are precarious, and so the nation that starts this process may have major responsibility for the annihilation of populations. If this should take place there might not be many who would be living, and articulate enough, to charge those responsible with guilt. The vast catastrophe would almost

[18] *On Escalation*, pp. 94-95.
[19] Morton Halperin, *China and the Bomb*, p. 67.

be beyond the comparative judgments of more guilt or less guilt. But, in advance, such judgments do have meaning in God's sight. The churches should so teach that they have meaning now as a mark of our humanity.

Today the danger of the use of nuclear weapons by the United States may be greater in Asia than in Europe. Our strategists should never forget the dimension of moral horror and of resentment at the thought that white men should think of Asians again as targets for nuclear bombs. To use them on helpless nations might win some quick military victories, but it would be a moral and a political disaster. Our claims as defenders of freedom could hardly survive such a disaster; we would stand out as the most feared representatives of ruthless power. Here we see clearly how technical and strategic decisions can be not only morally wrong but disastrously self-defeating, if they are not governed by political wisdom informed by moral sensitivity.

Preservation of moral inhibitions against being destroyers of other people needs special emphasis today both for its own sake and as one factor in preventing the most destructive deeds. It may well be a very effective factor when we stop thinking of the absolute enemy. I regard this chapter and the preceding one as belonging together, because, as we emerge from the Cold War, there is greater hope of moral restraint and of survival. Also, great attention must be given to alternatives to war and to the development of the institutions of world order. This will be the subject of the next chapter.

When nations are caught as they are today in a moral trap in connection with the structure of deterrence, this fact should bring upon them the strongest possible moral pressure both to find ways of reducing tensions and of limiting the danger of nuclear war under existing conditions and to change the conditions by seeking radical disarmament and institutional alternatives to violence.

6: *International Goals—Illusions and Hopes*

WE CANNOT deduce a secure view of the future of man in history from Christian teaching, but Christians should face the future with hope as well as with a sense of the precariousness of all human achievements. There is an irrational protection, which may be necessary if we are to act at all, against having to face with full imagination all of the cumulative dangers and possibilities of destruction that the future may hold. It is not easy to live with what we see in terms of the future destructiveness and the availability of nuclear weapons; if we add to these all other horrendous weapons that are possible, we might be obsessed by a nightmare. To glance at these more distant dangers is necessary, and yet there is practical validity in the maxim of Jesus, "Sufficient unto the day is the evil thereof." Concentration on what our generation may do and faith in God's ultimate rule over his creation, in his redemption of the person and in his over-ruling historical providence, are enough. This faith cannot be spelled out in concepts or pictures, and attempts to do so raise more problems than they solve. But human beings, who live brief lives and whose predictions of the distant future are usually hopelessly wrong, cannot take responsibility for that future. They do what they can in their own time and place, and beyond that they see through a glass darkly. If they are Christians, they live by proximate hopes and by an ultimate faith that is a gift of grace. This chapter is about proximate hopes. The proximate hope for the nations at this moment may be seen in the convergence of the moral pressures that cause nations to seek new forms of international community and the conditions that are necessary for survival.

Christian hope for the nations depends upon belief in the unity of humanity as created in the image of God and as the object of God's redemption in Christ. Time was when these two affirmations were in conflict, for theologians have used the very grace of God as one more basis for dividing humanity between the "ins" and the "outs," between us and them, between the saved and the lost. In the context of our hope for society, it is not necessary to take any position on the vexed question concerning a dogmatic universalism. It is enough to repudiate two distortions of Christian teachings. One has been the tendency in effect to draw lines that divide people in Christian terms that, with few exceptions, correspond to continents and cultures. It is easy to see the effect of such a division of humanity on the future of the nations. The contrast between Christendom and all of the rest of mankind has largely gone. It has certainly gone as a basis for pretensions. Also, Christian theologies have abandoned, by imperceptible stages and without many announcements, the separation of men into distinguishable groups of saved and lost. Christian teaching, both Protestant and Catholic, today has removed the obstacles to seeing the dignity and the integrity of non-Christians. There are no theologically or ecclesiastically determined boundaries to the saving grace of God. The Vatican Council, in its positive attitude toward non-Christians, may not have added anything to Catholic teaching, but it has altered the balance within that teaching. Both liberal and post-liberal Protestant theology, not least the theology of Karl Barth, stress this same openness to all humanity. This changed Christian thinking has great importance for genuine acceptance of a pluralistic world, and when relations with Communist nations become normal it will enable Christians to live with the people in them who have inherited the Communist prejudice against Christianity.

The relation between pluralism and relativism, between openness to people in other religious communities and belief that there is religious truth to be taken seriously, is an everyday problem for citizens of a religiously pluralistic nation, for those who combine faithfulness to the Christian revelation with full respect for their neighbors who reject it or who do not even find it interesting. On an international scale, the problem may not be different in principle, but it has vaster proportions.

Also, we should be clear about the danger of a debilitating

relativism when it comes to doctrines that are incompatible with the unity of humanity which Christians see from one point of view and in which others often believe with somewhat different presuppositions. There are morally poisonous doctrines that have their believers. Doctrines of white supremacy have flourished and, while under strong attack, still flourish in some Christian circles. The Christian religion is so many-sided that when some facets of it are taken out of context and distorted they can be used to give religious support to racial prejudice, economic exploitation, and total war. It is no wonder that protest sometimes comes in the form of atheism.

It is difficult to find the optimum point at which openness to others and faithful to one's own convictions meet. I doubt if it can be located theoretically or in terms of a general formula. Christians should not be inhibited in saying what they see to be true or in making their own contribution anywhere in the world. They should give themselves to the service of others, moved by the faith that those others and they themselves are loved of God and all are in need of his mercy. Nor should they hold themselves back from criticizing the irrelevance or inhumanity of any religious traditions or institutions, including some aspects of their own, so long as they try to understand before they criticize.

In the Christian tradition, beginning with Paul's verses about obedience to the governing authority (Romans xiii), there has been great stress upon the claims of political order. In general, order has been overstressed at the expense of justice and freedom in the traditional teaching of the great churches. The political authority and claim to obedience of rulers of various kinds have had more than enough support. In the modern period, this has been true of the national state; order and authority have had more emphasis than has transforming justice influenced by love for the neglected and exploited people. Today two changes are needed that are not easily reconciled in detail. One is the need for international order. All the claims for the role of Christian emperors, feudal rulers, or national states can be made in behalf of the developing institutions of the international community. At the same time, there needs to be far more emphasis than ever on what I call transforming justice, on the claims of the vast multitude of hungry and neglected people. Much of the tumult of our time that interferes with the development of world order, that makes for instability, comes from revolutionary movements and regimes that are associated with Communism or that frighten the guardians of stability because Communists may capture them. All of us live close to the tumult, and we live with the necessity of finding a way to institutions of order and peace on a world scale.

One of the most common expressions of the need for world order has been interest in proposals for world government. It is always amazing to me how many very able minds assume that what is rationally necessary is historically feasible soon, that the very announcement of the necessity can almost neutralize the many stubborn factors that prevent minimal mutual trust between many nations. It is assumed that the insecurity of all efforts to achieve peace in the face of the nuclear threat will drive mankind to choose what is rational: a supernational government under world law. As I have already said, I think there is power in this sense of what is necessary for survival, but I am compelled to believe, by what I see in the world today, that the nations will have to take much more modest steps toward the establishment of world order.

Before giving my reasons for this conclusion, I shall mention briefly one of the proposals for world government that is carefully worked out in considerable detail in the volume, *World Peace Through World Law* by Grenville Clark and Louis B. Sohn.[1] So complete is this scheme for world government as an alternative to the present partial anarchy that Herman Kahn suggested that the morning after the first "city exchange," a bloodless expression for the bloody destruction of cities in the United States and the Soviet Union, "The President of the United States might send a copy of this book to Premier Khrushchev saying: 'There is no point in your reading this book; you will not like it any more than I did. I merely suggest that you sign it, right after my signature. This is the only plan that has

[1] *World Peace Through World Law,* Harvard University Press, 1958.

been even roughly thought through; let us therefore accept it. We surely do not wish to set up a commission to set up other methods of organizing the world, because within weeks both of us will be trying to exploit our common danger for unilateral advantages. If we are to have a settlement, we must have it now, before the dead are buried.' " [2] This is a great tribute to the book, and it is a dramatic way of stating the difficulty in securing agreement on this or any other scheme, for the moment of real openness and repentance is likely to be short. Such a book as this will make its contribution to future discussion of the development of a world political authority. It is significant that Professor Sohn himself has been the author of particular schemes for inspection, in the case of disarmament agreements, that have entered into the actual negotiations between the United States and the Soviet Union.

The Clark-Sohn scheme is not intended to set up a worldwide administration concerned about the internal problems of nations. It is intended to deal only with the prevention of war. It is a system of enforceable world law in this limited context. It presupposes the disarmament of all nations. It presupposes almost universal membership with the denial of the right of withdrawal. It would create a General Assembly in which votes would depend on population, though this plan does give the same number of votes to all nations with populations of more than 140,000,000. China and India would have the same number of votes as the United States and the Soviet Union. It also involves an executive council, a court of law, and the continuation of the economic and social council of the United Nations.

I doubt very much if such a world government can be created by a decisive act of constitution-making. No political fiat can alter the location of national forms of power. Perhaps if things had fallen just right, the United States and the Soviet Union might have imposed such a government when they had a monopoly of nuclear power. But an agreement to do it would have been a miracle. It is one of the oddities of recent history

[2] Quoted in Paul Ramsey, *The Limits of Nuclear War*, Pamphlet published by Council on Religion and International Affairs, pp. 26-27.

that before Russia achieved nuclear strength, Bertrand Russell proposed that the United States use the threat of nuclear attack to compel the Russians to accept the Baruch plan.[3]

Reinhold Niebuhr, in his famous essay on the illusions of world government, is right in his main contention that governments have only limited efficacy in creating the community on which they depend for viability.[4] As he put it: "Virtually all arguments for world government rest upon the simple proposition that the desirability of world order proves the attainability of world government. Our precarious situation is unfortunately no proof, either of the moral ability of mankind to create a world government by act of will, nor of the political ability of such a government to integrate a world community in advance of a more gradual growth of 'social tissue' which every community requires more than government." [5]

Niebuhr does admit there are three types of "social tissue" that exist to a limited extent, and the international institutions that are possible depend upon their development. He refers to the following: economic interdependence, fears of mutual annihilation, and what he calls "an inchoate sense of obligation that transcends the nation." This inchoate sense of obligation is limited in its efficacy in relation to particular issues because of genuine disagreement concerning implications of obligation for policy. I think we can hope that reductions of the Cold War tensions which have moralistic overtones will increase the power and

[3] Christopher Driver, *op. cit.*, p. 18.

[4] It is interesting to observe that on this issue there was a united influence on the American churches by two men who were poles apart on most issues: Reinhold Niebuhr and John Foster Dulles. Mr. Dulles, who was at his best in his leadership of the churches during the Second World War in their preparation for peace, emphasized the policy of beginning with the existing United Nations, which was the war alliance, and expanding it, rather than attempting to leap into a completely new and universal political organization. He was a most effective link between the Protestant churches and the San Francisco conference at which the United Nations was founded. His political realism, though differently grounded than Niebuhr's, had in this respect some of the same effects.

[5] Reinhold Niebuhr, *Christian Realism and Political Problems*, Charles Scribner's Sons, 1953, p. 17.

scope of this inchoate sense of obligation. But the difficulty that is present in agreeing on the meaning of obligation is illustrated by the very sharp difference of opinion about the obligation of the United States in South East Asia, a difference of opinion within the United States itself as well as among the nations.

The revolutionary stirring within Asia and Africa and Latin America is almost sure to make all of these neat schemes of world government unacceptable. The fact that, in their scheme for weighted voting based on population, Clark and Sohn assign the same representation in the Assembly to all nations with more than 140,000,000 people reveals the problem. That very scheme was written from the point of view of the white Western world. How could we expect China and India to accept it or, if they did, to live with it very long? The effort to change it would threaten the balance of forces and be regarded by the powers that are now dominant as a revolutionary threat.

One of the chief reasons why such schemes are problematic is that even if a world government could be set up with something like a monopoly of decisive military power, including nuclear power, would there not be a continuous effort on the part of dissatisfied nations or groups of nations to snatch control of the levers of power in that world government? There would here be dangers of world-wide tyranny, of new forms of the threat of nuclear blackmail.

A civil war within this structure might be less lethal for humanity than a war under present conditions between two groups of nations with undiminished armaments. The experience of our own reasonably well-ordered federal government in the war between the states and even more recent difficulties in securing compliance with federal law from recalcitrant states illustrate the problem. The expression *world law* is used so much as pointing to a saving solution, but there are very great hurdles between our present situation and the willingness of powerful states to put themselves under an enforceable system of law that would hold, even when they believed that their vital interests or their ways of life might be threatened.

The great encyclical of Pope John XXIII, *Pacem in Terris,*

much as it is to be welcomed for its actual healing influence in the world, is completely lacking in any indication of how the world moves from the present situation to an international order that "corresponds to the objective requirements of the universal human good."

The Pope says: "Just as within each political community the relations between individuals, families and intermediate associations and public authority are governed by the principle of subsidiarity, so too the relations between the public authority of each political community and the public authority of the world community must be regulated by the same principle." "Must be" are words that hide an ocean of difficulties. "Subsidiarity" is the technical term used in Catholic political philosophy to refer to a right ordering of higher and lower units of community or the relation between private and public authorities, but it is very fluid. One might say that the whole question of states' rights versus federal authority in the United States has to do with the interpretation of the principle of subsidiarity, but the principle in itself in practice settles nothing; the issues are finally settled by power which now within the American system has enough moral authority to elicit substantial consent.

I see illustrated here a very important difference between Catholic and Protestant tendencies of thought. Protestants tend to stress the tragic irrationalities and the sinful stubbornness of men both personal and corporate. There is a tendency, on the other hand, in Catholic utterances to announce what is rational, what the moral law is, and to give the impression that the embodiment of the rational and the moral in human institutions and communities is not very difficult or far away. Indeed, the announcement seems almost to summon it into existence.

Readers may observe in this book a tendency, which they may regard as too optimistic, about the breaking through of the human in man in spite of ideologies and systems that confine and distort it. I am able to see the end of the Cold War. But this optimism does not imply optimism about the capacity of man to develop rational structures of order and to maintain them. To a degree, this is present, but it is always threatened by inner corrosion and by the emergence of new vitalities that had not been taken into account. I see a world that has great openness in it, a world of new possibilities, of new expressions of the human, of many hopes, but also a world of new conflicts, of new revolutions, of unexpected corruptions and hazards. And in the midst of this open world, I hope and pray for structures of world community that take into account the stubborn realities of power, of human differences, of conflicts of interest, of sin and irrationality. I hope for new providential neutralizing of some of these destructive tendencies, for new healing powers, for new effects of redemption even within the political order. But it will always be an untidy situation, in comparison with the great schemes for world order that are often projected.

These considerations lead me to give attention now to the United Nations. I believe that the United Nations is of great significance because it does not pretend to be an over-all solution to the problems of world order. It is inadequate from the point of view of collective security, but it is better suited to the realities with which we must live than are more ambitious and more consistent schemes. At the same time, it is open-ended and it has the capacity to consolidate gains that may be made on many levels. I have learned a good deal from the book by Professor Inis L. Claude to which I have referred, *Power and International Relations*. He puts the role of the United Nations very well when he says: "As a matter of fact, the primary political function of the United Nations is to help us to make the best of it." [6]

The United Nations is attacked from all sides. Many internationalists attack it for its weakness, for being paralyzed by the veto, for not being able to enforce its decisions, for not being a world government. It is quite true that it lacks an independent base for power that enables it to discipline stronger members. It is attacked by some Americans because it includes Communists and other foreigners. Since the United States can no longer command a majority in the Assembly, it is regarded by some Americans as primarily a threat to American aims and policies. It is attacked or at least downgraded by some more thoughtful Amer-

[6] Claude, *op. cit.*, p. 280.

icans who would give greater weight to a concert of like-minded powers than to the United Nations. But actually one of the remarkable facts about the United Nations is that there is a very widespread, wistful belief in it in the United States. Public-opinion polls show this, year after year, in spite of reasons for disappointment concerning its capacity to deal with the most threatening issues of this period. The churches have done a great deal, first to create and then to nourish this American belief in the United Nations. Sometimes churches concentrate on this subject because it is in church circles relatively non-controversial. It enables them to give attention to international relations and to satisfy the very great moral idealism in the churches without having to discuss the hard Cold War problems which are touched only marginally by the United Nations. This is partly a criticism, but I am very thankful for the extent to which the churches have kept the United Nations before their constituencies and helped to resist the type of American nationalism that regards the organization as an alien force in our midst.

As I have said, the United Nations is adapted to existing realities. One ground for saying this is that it reflects the world as it is, the distribution of economic, military, territorial, and demographic power. The great exception to such a statement is the absence of China. These forms of power are where they are. They cannot be relocated by any organization or by legal fiat. They can be put in a frame that makes some difference to the way in which they are used. It is both the weakness and the positive value of the United Nations that it cannot of itself settle the most vital issues that separate the great powers. If a majority of the Security Council could make the United Nations act as an instrument of collective security against the Soviet Union or against the United States, the organization would probably be destroyed, or it might become one side in a world war. The action in Korea was a special case—it was possible because of the absence of the Soviet Union—and it did not deal with a matter of security vital to any of the great powers, including the Soviet Union.

If it becomes possible to reduce conflicts between the great powers, the United Nations may well enter a new stage of effectiveness. But there are obstacles here over which it cannot leap, though they may be lowered by such historical developments as the reduction of tensions between the United States and the Soviet Union.

One area in which decisions reached outside the processes of the United Nations might greatly change its role is disarmament. At present, the powers go through so many motions about disarmament with little to show for them except the partial test ban treaty. No one knows when a breakthrough may come. Progress toward disarmament will depend not on any one factor but on at least three factors as they interact with each other. One factor is the reduction of the hostilities and fanaticism of the Cold War. If my fourth chapter contains much truth, the outlook for this is far from hopeless. A second factor is emphasis on restraints in the use of weapons, even in thinking about the use of weapons, which may come as an internal discipline in the most powerful countries. A third factor is the establishment of various kinds of peace-keeping machinery that can provide a degree of security to take the place of the security provided by national armaments. I cannot say that as of now the prospects for this are very hopeful, though there has been a beginning in the use of United Nations forces to keep the peace. Any progress that is made toward disarmament would interact positively with these factors that I have mentioned. We need to see all of these tendencies together and keep working on them all at once. Whenever there are any breakthroughs in regard to disarmament, the United Nations is always there to provide machinery to implement and police agreements. Indeed, I believe it is by some such route as this that institutions of world government may emerge. Thinking about ambitious proposals is not wasted time, because this can prepare for later steps; but we are not likely to move into world government by a series of major, constitutional decisions. We are more likely to do so by arriving at solutions of particular problems and then lodging responsibility for implementation with the United Nations.

So much for a glance at possible later developments. I want now to sketch briefly what I see to be the present contributions of the United Nations.

1. The Charter is an expression of moral and legal principles to which nations are committed. We cannot count on obedience to them, but it is possible to put nations on the defensive when they violate them. The Charter projects a relevant common-ground morality that can be a rallying point for the world. That may sound too idealistic, but I have in mind the verbalizing in the Charter of what may be no more than Reinhold Niebuhr's "inchoate sense of obligation that transcends the nation," to which I have referred. There are moral resources in Marxism that ultimately keep the Cold War from being an absolute moral conflict. These moral resources may be released in a constructive way, as the countries with Marxist creeds lose hardness and ruthlessness in regard to the means that go with revolutionary fanaticism. It is difficult for Americans to speak of such a thing for there is such a national obsession about Marxism and Communism that in effect we lack freedom of speech on the subject. George Kennan spoke out frankly and courageously in an address at the conference on *Pacem in Terris* in 1965. He said: "We impute to the Soviet leaders a total inhumanity not plausible even in nature, and out of accord with those humane ideals which we must recognize as lying together with other elements less admirable in the eyes of some of us, at the origins of European Marxism." The very conflict of values, which today may cause many readers to dismiss the moral and legal principles of the Charter as so much papering over of a limitless moral chasm, will not necessarily be the last word so far as the differences between the Communist and non-Communist nations are concerned.

The Charter can be understood as representing international positive law, as a modern *ius gentium* that depends upon the decisions of nations. But it is also possible to see this as an expression of a dynamic natural law of justice and order and humaneness. Protestants whose theology is opposed to stereotypes of natural law must still recognize the reality of a common-ground morality that unites people of different faiths and commitments.

There is a fascinating passage in the *Ethics* of Dietrich Bonhoeffer, one of the chief theological critics of the tradition of natural law. Bonhoeffer speaks of the correspondence between the second table of the Ten Commandments and what he calls "the law of historical life itself known to pagan governments." [7] Surely there is here a substitute for the concept of "natural law," and I think of the Charter as being in part at least an expression of this.

The dynamic aspect of this natural law or common-ground morality or this "law of historical life itself" may be seen at many points in the Charter but especially in its commitment to human rights and fundamental freedoms "without distinction as to race, sex, language, or religion" (Article 76). One of the principles of the Charter that expresses a high morality is its insistence "that the interests of the inhabitants of these territories [non-self-governing territories] are paramount" when they are administered by members of the United Nations. The Charter not only exalts peace but it also exalts the well-being of peoples as a responsibility of the powerful.

2. The United Nations is an instrument of continuous diplomacy. It makes it possible for the representatives and often the actual leaders of the nations to know each other, to meet under many informal as well as formal circumstances, to discuss, without publicity and fanfare, issues that may be very hot. There is a point at which the results of diplomacy should be open, but during the processes of negotiation there should be ample chance for tentative explorations that put no one on the spot, that commit no one to public positions from which it is difficult to depart.

Dr. Kenneth Thompson has emphasized this role of the United Nations in the following passage: "Parliamentary diplomacy can also help to keep open the channels between rival powers in world politics. The leaders of the Great Powers may in speeches, press conferences, or interviews give the signal they are prepared to negotiate. Then, within or outside the United Nations, alert diplomats move to explore the prospects of agreement. The classic case is of course the settlement of the Berlin blockade in 1948-1949 when United States Ambassador Philip C. Jessup success-

[7] Macmillan, 1955, p. 305.

fully explored with his Soviet colleague at the U.N. the meaning of a conciliatory statement by Soviet Premier Joseph Stalin. Thus far, diplomacy in the conference rooms and anterooms of the United Nations has filled in the gaps in contacts between adversaries in the Cold War. Is it too far-fetched to ask whether the United Nations may in the future provide opportunities for unobtrusive diplomatic contacts for countries separated by conflicts not between East and West but between North and South?" [8]

3. The United Nations is a precarious bridge between the two worlds that are in conflict. It is fortunate that the Russians and the nations of Eastern Europe are there. It is a great handicap that Communist China is not there. This would be only one aspect of the restoration of relationship between China and the international community, but an essential one. It is unfortunate that the United States has staked its prestige on this issue both at home and within the United Nations. The vote in 1965 in the Assembly on the relation of Communist China to the United Nations and the accompanying debate indicate that the United States will have to change its position or be outvoted in the near future.

4. The United Nations is a forum where world opinion can be developed, heard and focused. "World opinion" is an exaggerated expression, but it is not without meaning. What does take place is a general airing of a problem with many minds working on it; consequently, it is seen from many points of view. There may be real clarification of issues and some modification of the tendency toward polarization. This exposure of an issue and of the facts surrounding it is often a restraining factor. It gains time and puts all sides on the defensive.

One aspect of this process is that it gives real weight to the able representatives of smaller and middle-sized powers. They count as mediators and also as minds that provide ingenuity and wisdom. The Secretaries-General themselves have always come from such powers and their opportunities to take initiative have been one of the unexpected resources of the United Nations. The very

[8] "The New Diplomacy and the Quest for Peace" in *International Organization,* Volume XIX, Number 3, 1965, p. 408.

atmosphere of the United Nations favors restraint, and kudos goes to men who help to keep the peace.

5. The United Nations has an essential role—and an unexpected role so far as its importance is concerned—in giving status and international experience to the many new nations and their representatives. If it did not exist, something would have to be devised for this purpose alone. It gives these new nations a chance to express themselves and to learn the facts of international life. It provides a kind of public registry of national existence. It makes possible many forms of multilateral help for such nations, help that does not have on it the stamp of colonialism.

6. The United Nations provides even now a structure in which nations can move away from unilateral policies. This may be forced upon smaller powers but the great powers may accept multilateral disciplines as an honorable and face-saving way of getting out of an impasse. There is the possibility that the United States may be willing to allow its policy in Vietnam to be judged by the international community, perhaps by a conference that the United Nations may bring into being. Great powers at this stage may accept such multilateral judgment of their action and determination of their policies only as a last resort, but in the case of Vietnam it is becoming clearer every day that even successful unilateral action will only plunge the United States into deeper difficulty as the successor of other Western imperial powers in Asia.

7. The United Nations has already acted in relation to a number of international crises to keep the peace, to separate the two sides, and to make possible a provisional settlement. Korea was a special case, as I have said, but it did set an example of decisive multilateral action to resist aggression, and it had quite broad support until the crossing of the 38th parallel. The United Nations force that acts as a buffer between Israel and Egypt prevents overt violence and may well be a model for a type of action that stops shooting, prevents escalation, and gains time. The operation in the Congo was more ambiguous in its political objectives. A recent study of it by Ernest Lefever concludes that on balance it was a contribution to the peace and security of Central

Africa.[9] Also, Dr. Lefever emphasizes the surprising degree of unity within the United Nations force, gathered from many nations, and its development of an international ethos. These are only a few examples of concrete action by the United Nations, and it is significant that no one of them involved a life-and-death issue between the great powers.[10]

8. I need only refer to the activities of the specialized agencies and of various allied agencies that provide many services to nations in the sphere of welfare and economic development on a multilateral basis. This work of the United Nations may well expand and become the major channel of assistance for the so-called developing nations if such assistance becomes less important as an expression of Cold War rivalry.

These comments that I have made on the contribution of the United Nations, as it is, need to be seen in the context of what I have said about the open-ended character of the United Nations and its capacity to take on new functions, as these are delegated to it, even forms of authority over the nations that it does not now possess. Whenever agreements between nations are achieved and if the great powers now in conflict arrive at solutions, for example, in the case of disarmament, the United Nations can have a great role in implementing them and stabilizing them, and in so doing it will strengthen itself as a resource for peace and justice. Those who put their trust in the creation of full-orbed rational institutions will find this prospect bleak, but I believe that what I have suggested is closer to the way in which political institutions grow.

The development of international political institutions will depend in considerable measure on the formation of many non-political ties between the nations. Between some nations these al-

[9] *Crisis in the Congo,* The Brookings Institute, 1965, p. 181.
[10] While it is too early to assess the outcome of the initiative of the United Nations in ending hostilities between India and Pakistan in September 1965, this may be one of the greatest successes. The case was made to order for the United Nations, because the nations involved, which happen to be responsive to world opinion, had neither the will nor the resources for a long war and because the United States and the Soviet Union were on the same side.

ready are rich and have a long history. Associations of those who share common cultural and professional interests; exchange of students and teachers; trade and economic relationships, especially when there is some mutuality about them; cooperative efforts to deal with such problems as hunger and disease, the conditions of labor and the coping with the weather; movements of persons and friendships across boundaries—these and many other types of human contacts form the substance of international life. They should be seen against the background of a common fate and some widely held if not universal convictions about what is good for man in spite of ideological and religious differences. There will be bitter enmities, explosive rebellions, dangerous stalemates, but the hope is that these will not always divide humanity at the center and that they can be surrounded and absorbed by a wider community and that, even when there is violent conflict, it can be limited. Even now, there is hope in the mutual support between the good that should draw nations together and the conditions for their survival.

The church as an international community is one of the ties that binds together people who are citizens of many nations. In an earlier chapter, I emphasized the reality of the church as an essential element of the Christian perspective. In the next chapter, I shall deal more concretely with the church as a factor in international relations and in the formation of foreign policy in some nations.

7: The Role of the Church

First thoughts about the role of the church in relation to international relations and foreign policy may be reflections on the failure of the church—its irrelevance, its default, even its apostasy. The church has failed to prevent the fratricidal wars of Christendom, and in past centuries churches have inspired their own religious wars, both against infidels and against each other. The close tie between churches and states and churches and nations has generally robbed the churches of their ethical independence in times of conflict. Lip service to the idea of the just war has seldom caused a national church to regard the cause of its own nation as unjust. There have been limitations of conflict both in terms of the forms of violence and in the treatment of the defeated enemy, but these limits have not been maintained as whole populations have become emotionally involved and have been overwhelmed by the technology of weapons. There was one gain between the First and Second World Wars: churches in the earlier war were more uncritical supporters of their nations than they were in the later one. An important minority among churchmen in Germany opposed Hitler's war, and churches among the Western allies, while supporting the war against the Nazis, did not regard the military aspect of the war as a holy crusade, as they were inclined to do in the First World War. Churches in the Second World War were more reserved in identifying the symbols of the faith with the military side of national life. No one was more opposed to the Nazis than the Archbishop of Canterbury, William Temple, and on theological principle he rejected pacifism. Yet, as Archbishop, he spoke out against prayers for victory. He wrote: "It is, I think, far better not to pray directly for victory at all. But it is permissible, though not free from spiritual danger, if we add and mean the words, 'if it be thy will.' " [1] There were continual discussions both in Britain and in the United States about the differences between calling the war "just" and calling it "holy." There was a general preference for "just," and yet this was seen in the context of the need of a common repentance on both sides.[2]

When we are thinking of the ethical failures of the church, it is always sobering to me to realize that in the case of so many social evils, while there is a Christian inspiration behind much of the struggle against them, the church as an institution is always slow to grasp the issue and slow to act. Churches in the United States did not speak with a clear voice about slavery until it ceased to exist. Now they are unanimously opposed to slavery! They were slow in responding to the evil in racial segregation; now they are clear about this in all of their official and unofficial teaching that has more than local influence.

I take for granted all that can be said in criticism of the slowness of the church to respond to the great moral issues of our time. But this book is based also on the assumption that there has been much sharpening of the social conscience of the church in recent decades, that within the denominations and the ecumenical structures, new possibilities have emerged. This chapter is concerned with these new possibilities rather than with laments about either past or present failures.

In this context, the church has two major roles. It lives and speaks and acts as a universal community relating Christians to each other across most of the international boundaries that separate them. It lives and speaks and acts as a community within each nation and it should seek to bring Christian guidance and influence to bear on the attitude of the nation and the policies of the government. I have already indicated that there are limits to the competence of churches in advising their members or governments about policy, but they should become far better pre-

---

[1] *Thoughts in War Time*, Macmillan, London, 1940, pp. 43-44.
[2] I have summarized the discussion of these issues in the period of the Second World War in my *Christians and the State*, Charles Scribner's Sons, 1958, pp. 175-180.

pared than they are to give the guidance that is in their province.

The first role may generally be more a matter of being than of doing, or more a by-product of what the church should continually be doing than a specific activity planned to influence the relations of nations. Yet there are some strategies of the churches that have immediate relevance. There is the sending of people from one nation to another as a part of the mission of the church. There is the sending of material aid from church to church. There are many meetings of churchmen from two or more nations to discuss together the problems that may unite or separate them. There are innumerable activities of the ecumenical institutions that bring together Christians across national and cultural boundaries, some of them directly related to international issues such as those arranged by the Church Commission on International Affairs, the agency of the World Council of Churches, and many others that may not be focused on this subject but which strengthen the mutual understanding of churches with one another. When the activities of the Protestant and Orthodox churches are added to those of Roman Catholics from many nations, I see an amazing network of international activities and relations under the auspices of the church.

It is difficult today to do justice to the mighty effort of foreign missions that established churches and many other Christian institutions in most of the countries of Asia, Africa, and Latin America. The reality of the world-wide church is the fruit of this missionary work. The identification of life with life across boundaries of nation and culture was a remarkable demonstration of Christian faith and love and responsibility. It is easy now to see the faults of this enterprise, to recall the many pretentious Western claims that accompanied it, to emphasize the paternalism and the social blind spots that a sincere Christian impulse did not erase. Much that was done belonged to its time, and that time has gone; there was a failure to prepare for the days of revolution, independence, and nation-building. The missionary himself usually has had to be non-political as he was the guest of the nation or of the colonial government, and so he tended to encourage a non-political attitude in the churches under his influence. Today the churches are there. They still need help from the older churches. The contemporary missionary usually works under the indigenous church that he serves, and one of the main results of his presence is to help preserve ties between old and new churches. The younger generation of Christians in the continents of the younger churches talk back to Western churches in no uncertain terms!

To indicate the way in which the churches during the Second World War on both sides of the conflict preserved a remarkable openness toward each other, I quote a paragraph of my own, written in 1944.[1] Nothing that I might write now could convey as well how it felt to live through those years as a member of the universal Church.

Most important of all has been the extent to which Christians on both sides of the line of battle have retained a sense of belonging to the same Church. The experience of the Church in this war has been quite different from its experience in the First World War. Though this war reflects a far deeper conflict within humanity than the earlier struggle, it has actually less seriously divided the Church. One reason for this is the very fact of the deep conflict within humanity (not identical with the international struggle) and the discovery that in that conflict large groups of Christians in Germany are on the side to which we, too, belong. We know less about Japanese Christianity, and recently the Church in Japan has been seriously maligned by an American journalist. However, American churchmen who know Japanese Christianity best have confidence in the essential integrity of the Japanese Christians and believe that they will be one factor in the life of Japan that will be on the side of the kind of Japan with which the world can live. One of the most surprising evidences of the sense of belonging to the same Church which are now common among Christians, in spite of the war, is the story of collaboration between Christians in the German armies of occupation and the leaders of the churches in Norway and Holland and other countries in resistance to the Nazis. This is a story that is known to us here through the channels of the World Council of

[1] John C. Bennett, "The Protestant Churches and World Order," *World Order: Its Intellectual and Cultural Foundations*, ed. F. Ernest Johnson, Institute for Religious Studies, New York, Harper and Brothers, 1944, p. 126.

Churches but the details cannot yet be told. One of the marks of the kind of churchman who has not sold out to the Nazis in Germany is this desire to preserve a relationship with the Church beyond Germany. Hitler hoped to make the Church a mere tool of his policy, but he conspicuously failed.

At the end of the Second World War, the churches were a powerful factor in bringing together not only the Christians but the peoples of both sides. This was facilitated by the fact that an important part of the church in Germany opposed Hitler and his government, and even willed the defeat of Germany. Reconciliation between anti-Nazi Germans and Christians in the countries that had fought against Germany came quickly. Although issues were less clear, the reconciliation between Christians in Japan and American Christians began soon after hostilities had ceased. The Reconstruction Department of what was then "the World Council of Churches in process of formation" did a vast amount to heal the wounds of the war as it provided channels for the efforts of churches in many countries to help the victims of war. That so much destruction could be followed so soon by acts of reconciliation on both sides should be remembered as a great wonder.

The conflicts of the Cold War have separated churches from each other. In many cases sheer physical separation has been forced by governments. Communist governments during the revolutionary period resist the development of non-political relations between people across national boundaries. They fear ideological contamination. They keep religious institutions and leaders under strict control at home and allow only a few on whom they can count politically to travel. The very conception of the claims of an ecumenical church suggests to them only a political threat.

Very slowly some of these impediments to relations with Christians abroad are breaking down in Eastern Europe. The Soviet Union has allowed the Russian Orthodox Church to join the World Council of Churches, and this church retains continuous liaison with the World Council at the top level. Delegations of churchmen are exchanged between the Soviet Union and other countries, including the United States. There are many more contacts between Christians in some of the smaller European Communist countries and their fellow-Christians in the West, perhaps especially in the case of Czechoslovakia. Christians in China are almost entirely sealed off from such contacts, except for an occasional visit to a few Chinese leaders by churchmen from Western nations other than the United States. Churches in this country should continually seek ways by which relations with Christians in China can be re-established, but the initiative will probably have to come from ecumenical bodies or from churches in non-aligned nations. Relations with Christians in Cuba should be high on the agenda and since they have some freedom of movement, this should not be a great difficulty as the American obsession about Cuba subsides.

The World Council of Churches can do a great deal to restore relationship across the Cold War barriers. For years its conferences and Assemblies have facilitated this. Also many *ad hoc* meetings designed especially to promote understanding between Eastern and Western churchmen have been held. One of the most important of these was a meeting of a hundred theologians, church leaders, and laymen from twenty-eight countries of Europe and North America, with participants almost equally divided between Eastern and Western countries at the Ecumenical Institute near Geneva in 1965.

The World Peace Conference that meets in Prague every few years brings together Christians from both sides of the Iron Curtain. It has had a checkered history because in its earlier years it seemed to be chiefly a sounding board for Eastern propaganda, but the most recent meeting drew many Western Christians who would previously have shunned it. Its public discussions were franker and less one-sided, and it provided a unique opportunity for informal contacts.[2]

It will illustrate the kind of direct approach on matters of na-

[2] Professor Charles C. West has written a discriminating report of the "Second All-Christian Peace Assembly" that met in Prague in 1964. He emphasizes its positive role as a reconciling event in spite of some political ambiguities. He says, "This may well have been the largest and most varied body of Christians ever to meet in a land under Communist rule." See *Christianity and Crisis,* November 16, 1964.

tional policy by churches to one another to record that, during a period of a few weeks in the summer of 1965, there were four quite independent efforts by Christians in other countries to speak to Christians in the United States about American foreign policy. Four of the leading Protestants in Latin America sent to the American churches a message expressing the great shock that all of Latin America had experienced as a result of the precipitous landing of American marines in the Dominican Republic. The officers of the East Asia Christian Conference, an affiliate of the World Council of Churches, sent a message to the American churches strongly criticizing American policy in Vietnam. A delegation of Japanese Christians, who were leaders of the United Church of Christ in Japan, though they came unofficially, visited the United States and held meetings with American churchmen in several centers to share their grave misgivings concerning American policy in Vietnam. Notice that in each of these cases it was the churchmen from churches that had been founded by missionaries who expressed themselves so independently and frankly.

The fourth case was somewhat different because the initiative was taken by an agency of the World Council of Churches, of which American churches are members. The Church Commission on International Affairs, through its Executive Committee, in July 1965 spoke about the situation in Vietnam in a very circumspect manner, but the statement was, on the whole, critical of American policy, especially the unilateral character of the American intervention in Vietnam and the emphasis on military methods. A supplementary statement by the officers of this same Commission was definite in criticizing by implication the American policy of seeking to exclude mainland China from the United Nations.

I cite these four cases not to call attention to the content of the action but to illustrate the kind of procedure that we should expect in the relationship between churches. The fact that the policy of the United States was criticized in each case should be explained in part by the fact that of the powers that are now dominant in the world, the United States is the one in which such criticisms can be given most publicity and in which, so far as the churches are concerned, a sympathetic hearing can be expected. The ecumenical community will be fortunate and the world will be fortunate when equally frank speaking by churches to one another becomes possible in all directions. Such speaking should come out of a relationship of common faith and common obedience, of mutual respect and love.

In spite of the experience of listening to Christians in other countries when they criticize the foreign policy of one's own country, we can expect that, in most cases, Christians will defend the position taken by their own government in a crisis, perhaps the more so when it is attacked by foreigners. This is a "given" in most situations, but it is not unchangeable. Even when there is such natural self-defense, criticism without too much self-righteousness may affect the attitudes of those who receive it, even if it does not win full assent. The support of one's own nation by all of its citizens, Christians and others, may seem so natural that it calls for no explanation, but it is useful to distinguish the different motives that lie behind it. It may come from a passionate nationalism. It may come from a sincere identification of the nation with a cause that transcends the nation, whether it be the defense of Western values or democracy or the goals of social revolution. Often it may be little more than the tendency for any group to see more clearly its own side of a dispute when there are really two sides, a tendency strengthened by the limits of information and the pressure of national propaganda.

There have been notable cases of Christian minorities opposing their own country even in time of war, as a Christian minority did in Germany under Hitler. There have been notable cases of Christians who have opposed a particular policy of their government in wartime, as the Bishop of Chichester did in the House of Lords in his speeches against obliteration bombing of German cities in the Second World War. Many of the criticisms by American leaders of the policy of the United States in Vietnam should be mentioned. Criticism of national policy may at times be the best expression of loyalty to one's nation. Mutual questioning across national lines in the universal church should be emphasized before a crisis reaches a "point of no return," but the church must not give up, even when the obstacles are greatest. The ecumenical bodies, the Pope in his present role of active peace-maker, and churches in neutral nations should struggle to maintain contacts with both sides in a conflict. Churches need to raise up more statesmen of their own who, in their distinctive sphere of ecumenical relations, work both with Christian love and with sophistication about political issues to overcome the causes of war and to reconcile estranged and hostile peoples.

In discussing the second role of the church, I shall limit myself to what it may do in the United States. Many of the same things could be said, however, about other countries in which there is general freedom of expression and in which there are important Christian elements in the national tradition that enable the church to gain a hearing. I doubt if formal church-state relations are a decisive matter. Indeed, one of the chief problems of the church in this country is that, in spite of the legal separation of church and state, it may be taken into camp by a government that is basically friendly to churches and in which the policy-makers are in many cases loyal church members.

The deepest contribution of the church in relation to issues of foreign policy is for it to be itself and to mediate the gospel continually with all of its implications both to its own members and to all who are open to it in the nation. This does not mean that a conventional preaching of a personal gospel to individuals who are then expected to translate it into terms that are relevant to national decisions is enough. There are too many inherited blind spots and distortions in the church itself and there is too great pressure upon the Christian citizen to accept a picture of the world that supports national policy. The gospel needs to be interpreted in ways that are relevant to the international situation. The church has a special responsibility to counteract the way in which religion is often misused in public life to justify dominant public activities and national policies.

Much was learned during the Second World War by churches in the United States about how to speak and to act directly to help prepare the nation for the decisions that would come with peace. The Commission on a Just and Durable Peace, under the chairmanship of John Foster Dulles, did a great deal to prevent any possible development of post-war isolationism. Because of its work, the churches played an important part in securing general support for the United Nations and for many constructive international policies such as the Marshall Plan and Point Four. It is difficult to distinguish between the influence of the churches and the pressure of events that convinced people that these internationalist policies were in the national interest, but there is no doubt that the former was considerable. Ever since those early post-war years, the churches, through the National Council of Churches and through agencies of the denominations, have given strong support to these aspects of foreign policy.

The churches are in a favorable position to encourage throughout the nation widespread discussion of controversial issues that are difficult for most leaders in the community to touch. There have been periods of fear and conformism in connection with the discussion of the Cold War issues, especially in regard to China. The churches have helped to break the taboo about China, but the taboo about Cuba is still too much for them. For more than a decade, they have been remiss in dealing with the issues of nuclear policy and strategy, which I raised in an earlier chapter.

One method that the churches have used that has been especially fruitful has been the official calling of a conference or a consultation, asking such a body to speak for itself to the churches and the nation. This has been the pattern of six National World Order Study Conferences since 1942. These were called by the Federal Council of Churches and later by its successor, the National Council of Churches, with the full cooperation of the denominations. Between four and five hundred churchmen, mostly appointed by the denominations, have met under these auspices to discuss many of the most perplexing and controversial issues of foreign policy. The reports of these conferences have had a cumulative effect and, though they represent only those who were present at the conference, they do constitute a body of teaching within the churches, which has its own weight and which has been used systematically to stimulate further discussion throughout the country. The reports of the conferences are sometimes attacked, as in the case of a statement made at the Fifth World Order Study Conference at Cleveland in 1958. One paragraph, out of a long message, received most of the emphasis because it called for steps "toward the inclusion of the People's Republic of China in the United Nations and for its recognition by our government." The statement made clear that the recommendation was not unconditional, for it spoke of safeguarding "the rights of people of Taiwan and of Korea." For years this was a matter of major controversy, and the National Council was furiously attacked for allowing a conference, called under its auspices, to make such a statement. The General Board of the Council made clear that the statement was unofficial but stood by the right of the conference to make it. How could it bring together several hundred responsible people for several days and censor what they decided to say together? Moreover, this method has the value of making available the results of responsible corporate thinking without officially committing the churches. Such guidance is much needed, even when there is no consensus. To a certain extent the Cleveland Conference of 1958 broke the ice on this subject of American policy in regard to China and made it easier for others to say the same thing.[3]

[3] For example, in 1964 the International Convention of the Disciples of Christ and in 1965 the General Synod of the United Church of Christ passed resolutions calling for the admission of Communist China to the United Nations, without stirring much controversy. The Sixth World Order Study Conference, in St. Louis in October 1965, went beyond the much criticized conference in Cleveland in calling for many kinds of relationship with Communist China, and at this time the General Board of the National Council endorsed the substance of the Conference's recommendations on China.

It also passed a strong recommendation for the revision of policy in relation to Vietnam, including the halting of the bombing of North Vietnam for a long enough period to create more favorable circumstances for negotiations and for willingness to negotiate with the National Liberation Front.

This policy statement by the St. Louis conference on Vietnam was in substance approved by the General Board of the National Council of Churches. It has been published with a message to the churches by the General Board that states in the strongest terms the morally and politically self-defeating character of a long continued unilateral military action in Vietnam. Here

There are times when the churches should go beyond the stimulation of discussion and seek to develop at least a provisional consensus on particular issues of foreign policy. This is where the self-limitations of the churches should be emphasized. Such a consensus should not be the result of a kind of Gallup Poll of the constituency of the churches. The results of such a poll would hardly differ from a cross section of public opinion in the nation. Churches are popular and their local members reflect the social views of the professional and other social groups from which they come; they do not have a distinctive position as churches. Church opinion should be formed by processes that bring together both clergy and laity, persons of different social background and bias, experts in different fields in the context of the church, and this means in the context of the church's international experience. What comes out of continued discussions of this sort is different from a raw consensus that is obtained by random sampling of the church members as individuals. This process should be cumulative with a chance to check and re-check. The consensus at whatever level does not become for the members a law that defines their status as churchmen. There may be exceptions to this, as in the case of the attitude of Christians in Germany to the doctrines and practices of the Nazis. The kind of segregationism that would exclude persons of another race from a church might well be regarded as a sign of unfaithfulness. In the case of foreign policy, it is difficult to suggest comparable moral heresies that would make church discipline or perhaps self-exclusion appropriate. Heresies in this area might include the support of preventive war, or of the use of weapons of mass destruction against populations, or of the isolationism that refuses aid to the hungry parts of the world. I have no desire to suggest laws here

---

is one sentence: "We believe that if the United States follows a unilateral policy in Vietnam, no conceivable victory there can compensate for the distrust and hatred of the United States that is being generated each day throughout much of the world because we are seen as a predominantly white nation using our overwhelming military strength to kill more and more Asians." What the National Council of Churches has done about the war in Vietnam is a most important example of church action on foreign policy.

but only to indicate areas where churches may come to stand for something definite enough to cause self-exclusion by some of their members when they find themselves on the other side. I also have no desire to press this self-exclusion as something to be desired, because an individual might change if he remained in the church, or at least, his children might gain new convictions if his family remained in the church.

The consensus toward which a church or churches should work would seldom have to do with immediate tactics in foreign policy. The policy-makers may be in the church and their consciences and presuppositions should be formed under the influence of Christ—also the consciences and presuppositions of many of those who create the public opinion that sets limits to national policy. Central is the cultivation of sensitivity to what any policy does to people, to people on the other side of a conflict or to those who may be innocent bystanders. The presuppositions and the goals of policy should be kept under criticism, and people should be made aware of the special national temptations, enabling them to criticize American as well as Russian or British or Indian forms of self-righteousness. Churches have a chance, as I have said, to expose their members to the way in which the policies of their nation appear to people in other situations. This does not mean that everyone except the American government is right but that, especially in the midst of a crisis or tense situation, people need to be able to transcend the feelings and ideas by which they are surrounded. I think we have learned from the American experience in connection with Vietnam how quickly a tendency toward conformism develops, and how considerations that have great human importance, such as the effect of American bombings on the villages of South Vietnam, are played down in comparison with immediate military successes. One special responsibility of the churches is to guide the state concerning the misuse of religion, with churches themselves criticizing their own misuse of religion.

All that I have said so far has to do with pre-political guidance, with preparatory thinking to help those who must make the precise policies on the spot with information not available to churches. Professor Ramsey is so much impressed by the limits of the competence of the churches that he calls a halt here and asks the churches to "stand in awe before people called political 'decision makers' or rather before the majesty of topmost political agencies." [4] He is right in insisting that the church should normally emphasize the *perspectives* that guide policy-makers and the moral limits that they should observe; but what are the churches to do when they have observed the effects of wrong or dubious perspectives in the actual performance of policy-makers? What are they to do when the "magistrates" before whom they are asked to stand in awe are rigid, headstrong, or blind to the moral meaning of well known consequences of their decisions? In general, this separation of the "topmost political agencies" from the people from whom they come, to whom they are responsible, and by whom they are pushed in one direction or another is quite wrong. If the churches can criticize perspectives, they should be able to cry out against the end-product of the perspectives that they have criticized. This does not mean that they can project another policy in all its necessary details. It is a common mistake to assume that churches and also citizens in general should not criticize the policy of a government unless they can with confidence recommend an alternative policy. Usually only those who have responsibility on the spot can choose the immediate next steps involved in an alternative policy, but they may need to be prodded to do so by criticism of the presuppositions and known consequences of present policy.

Sometimes a nation comes to a fork in the road, when it must choose between policies that may have the most fateful results. A relatively non-controversial illustration of this was the decision of the Senate to ratify the partial test ban treaty. There were many highly technical issues wrapped up in that decision, and yet I believe that the churches were right in bringing pressure on the Senate to ratify the treaty. When there has been a long debate and when the issues have been shaken down, there must be a *yes* or a *no*. All the reservations that one may have, all the varied shades of support for or opposition to a position are silenced by an *either/or* that allows no *but*. There are risks here,

[4] *Christianity and Crisis*, June 28, 1965.

but the churches may run the greatest risk if they remain silent in fear of stepping out of their sphere.

Professor Gabriel Almond has written one of the most authoritative books on the forces that influence foreign policy, *The American People and Foreign Policy*.[5] In the original edition of the book in 1950, he makes the point that the great "majority of church organizations in the United States adhere to the foreign policy consensus." Then, he says of the Federal Council of Churches and the Catholic Association for International Peace that "the policies of both of these organizations are influenced by Christian pacifist attitudes which sometimes lead them to minimize military security consideration." This is, in his mind, a criticism, and he makes a similar criticism of the academic influences on foreign policy: "It is perhaps true that the secondary schools and most of the colleges tend to stress international organization and foreign policy idealism at the expense of security considerations." [6]

It is very instructive to note that Professor Almond, in a new edition of this book ten years later, makes the following complaint about the foreign policy of the decade of the fifties: "Our foreign policy turned into a hard shell of military production and deployments, security diplomacy and a program of foreign aid that was assimilated into our security diplomacy. The image we turned to the world was contaminated by internal distrust, arrogant self-righteousness, and shaky nerves productive of boasts and threats." [7] In other words, the ingredients most lacking in the foreign policy of the 1950s were the very ones that Professor Almond mildly criticized the churches and academic institutions for emphasizing too much in the previous period. We cannot deduce from this that military security will take care of itself. The churches ought not to give the impression that it is without ethical sanction. On the other hand, it is probably true that at the present time the tougher elements in foreign policy are so well established and have so much support from what President Eisen-

[5] Harcourt Brace, 1950
[6] *Ibid.*, p. 118.
[7] Praeger, 1960, p. xv.

hower in an inspired moment called "the military industrial complex" that the churches have been right in putting the emphasis on the elements which the government is most tempted to neglect.

Policies in the area of grave international conflict usually have two prongs: one involves the use of power that may or may not take the form of the application of military force; the other involves constructive and curative action, the preparation for a stage beyond sheer conflict, for negotiations, for peace and reconciliation. Any government is likely to be divided within itself so far as the emphasis on these two prongs is concerned. The churches are often needed to stress those aspects of policy which depend upon national self-criticism, upon openness to the needs of the people, upon the humanity of opponents, upon the obligation to find a way out of the self-defeating efforts to achieve security through nuclear deterrence in an unlimited arms race. When a nation is trapped so that all choices available are morally intolerable, this very situation becomes the source of an imperative to take a fresh view of the assumptions on which previous decisions have been made.

The recital of organizational attempts to relate Christians to each other across national boundaries and to influence the policies of governments, and the emphasis upon meetings and words suggest only the surface manifestation of what should be a far more pervasive reality. What the churches do officially is less important than the many unofficial initiatives within the Christian community that relate the gospel to the revolutionary struggles for justice and peace among the nations. Often these are on the fringe of the church even though they are in response to powers and influences of which the church has been the chief bearer in history. These initiatives should create an atmosphere in which it will be natural for the church as church to speak and act at a moment of national decision. There are indications that in the 1960s there are new expectations in the church and for the church. This is true of both Protestants and Catholics. We should not limit our initiatives to some fixed patterns of what seemed realistic or appropriate at another time. There is hope in the fact that the necessities for the survival of humanity correspond to the demands of the conscience. There should be, and I believe there will be, new thoughts, new beginnings, new social and political forms, new structures of the church. There lie ahead new possibilities as Communist and non-Communist nations, as affluent nations and nations that struggle against the poverty of the ages, experience the pressure of God that disturbs and corrects and redeems.